THE BASICS OF METALS AND METALLOIDS

CORE CONCEPTS

THE BASICS OF METALS AND METALLOIDS

KRISTA WEST

ROSEN
PUBLISHING®

New York

This edition published in 2014 by:

The Rosen Publishing Group, Inc.
29 East 21st Street
New York, NY 10010

Additional end matter copyright © 2014 by The Rosen Publishing Group, Inc.

Library of Congress Cataloging-in-Publication Data

West, Krista, author.
The basics of metals and metalloids Krista West.—First edition.
    pages cm.—(Core concepts)
Audience: Grades 7 to 12.
Includes bibliographical references and index.
ISBN 978-1-4777-2713-3 (library binding)
1. Metals—Juvenile literature. 2. Semimetals—Juvenile literature. I. Title.
TA459.W484 2014
546.3—dc23

                                                    2013027807

Manufactured in the United States of America

CPSIA Compliance Information: Batch #W14YA: For further information, contact Rosen Publishing, New York, New York, at 1-800-237-9932.

© 2007 Brown Bear Books Ltd.

CONTENTS

CHAPTER ONE

AN OVERVIEW OF METALS

Most elements are metals, and we see them all around us, from a paperclip to the wings of a jet aircraft. Metals also form many important compounds. These substances are used to make dyes and soaps. They even occur in our bodies.

Nearly three-quarters of all the elements on Earth are metals. Many of the most common elements are metals, and they have been used by humans for thousands of years. Today modern technology uses metals to make everything from skyscrapers and spacecraft to medicines and paints.

People first began using metals to make tools about 5,000 years ago. Historians call that time the Bronze Age, because most metal objects were made of bronze. Bronze is a mixture of two metals: copper and tin. Bronze objects are not very strong, but they still allowed people

Metal cans are prepared to be recycled. Metals are very useful substances and are found in all areas of everyday life.

to create a wide range of tools to help them survive.

From about 1900 BCE, people began using a harder metal called iron. The Iron Age had begun. Iron tools and weapons were harder and more useful than bronze ones. Civilizations that could use iron were more successful than those still using bronze. People armed with iron weapons were able to defeat fighters equipped with bronze weapons.

During the Iron Age there were many migrations (movements of people) across Asia and Europe. As people learned to use iron, their civilizations became more powerful. As a result they began to take over new areas of land—all thanks to a metal. Iron is still the most-used metal today. Ninety-five percent of all metal objects are made from iron.

THE WIDE WORLD OF METALS

There is no strict definition of a metal, but metals tend to have many similar properties: Metals are solid in normal conditions, and most only melt and boil at high temperatures. They are also shiny, flexible, and ductile—they can be stretched into thin wires. Metals are also good conductors. That is, they let electricity and heat pass through them quickly.

Of the 98 elements found naturally on Earth, 65 are metals. Iron (Fe) and nickel (Ni) are the most common metals on the planet. Earth's super-hot core is thought to be made of these metals. In the rocks of Earth's crust, aluminum (Al) is the most common, followed by iron,

CHEMISTRY IN ACTION
COLORFUL CHARACTER

Some uses of metals are obvious, like electric wires and the bolts holding cars together. Others are not so clear, like the metals contained in colored items, such as lipsticks, dyes, and paints. Many of these get their color from metals. Some metals produce many different pigments (colored substances). For example, chromium produces yellow, red, and green pigments.

The colors of many paints are produced by substances that contain metal atoms.

A statue made from bronze, a mixture, or alloy, of two metals—copper and tin. Bronze objects have been made for 5,000 years, and the alloy is still a useful material today.

semiconductors. A semiconductor only conducts electricity in certain conditions. At other times they are insulators—they block the flow of heat and energy.

GROUPING THE METALS

Because there are so many different types of metals on Earth, chemists organize them in groups according to their atomic structure and properties. This helps chemists predict how different metals will behave when they encounter other elements.

The easiest way to learn the different groups of metals is with a periodic table, an organized array of the elements.

sodium (Na), potassium (K), and magnesium (Mg). Like most other metals, these elements occur as ores. An ore is a natural compound, or mineral, that contains large amounts of a metal. (A compound is a substance that is formed when the atoms of two or more elements join during a chemical reaction.) A few metals, such as gold and silver, are found pure instead of as ores.

The other metals must be refined from ore. A refined metal has been purified to get rid of other unwanted elements. Once pure, most metals are then used in alloys. An alloy is a metallic substance that is made up of two or more metals mixed together. For example, brass is an alloy of copper and zinc.

Seven of the elements are considered metalloids. These are substances with properties of both metals and nonmetals. They are sometimes termed semimetals. Silicon (Si) is the most common metalloid. One thing that makes metalloids different is that many are

KEY DEFINITIONS

• **Alloy:** A metallic substance that contains two or more metals.

• **Metal:** An element that is generally solid, shiny, moldable, ductile, and conductive.

• **Metalloid:** A substance with properties of both a metal and a nonmetal.

• **Refine:** To purify a metal by getting rid of other unwanted elements.

• **Ore:** A mineral that contains valuable amounts of a metal.

CHEMISTRY IN ACTION

STARDUST

Scientists think that just three elements—hydrogen, helium, and lithium—were created 14 billion years ago in the first moments of the Big Bang. Hydrogen and helium gases were most abundant, but there were also tiny amounts of the metal lithium. Lithium is the lightest of all metals and also has the smallest atom. It floats in water and oil.

Lithium is the simplest metal. It is found in the huge clouds of gas and dust that form into stars.

The periodic table provides information about individual elements and groups of elements. Metals are found on the left-hand side of the table, and nonmetals on the right. Most elements are considered metals, so they spread more than halfway across the table.

The periodic table is used to show chemists trends among the elements. The most metallic elements are located in the bottom-left corner. The most nonmetallic ones are positioned in the upper-right corner. The boundary between metals and nonmetals is a diagonal line running through the left side of the table, from aluminum (Al) to polonium (Po).

In the periodic table elements are formed into columns. A column of elements is called a group. Each group has a number that shows where the column sits in the table.

The atoms of the members of a group have a similar structure. It is this structure that determines how an element will react and form bonds. This book examines five types of metals.

ATOMIC STRUCTURE

All elements, including the metals, are made of atoms. Atoms are the smallest pieces of an element that can retain the properties of that element. The structure of the atom is important because it determines how that element bonds with other elements. How an element forms bonds determines many of the properties of that substance. Let us back up a little and review the inside of the atom.

At the center of the atom is the nucleus, a dense ball of positively

Pure silicon looks a little like metal. However, this element is a metalloid, and it has some of the properties of both metals and nonmetals.

charged particles called protons and neutral particles called neutrons.

The protons give the nucleus a positive charge. Opposite charges attract each other, while the same charges repel (push away). As a result the nucleus attracts negatively charged particles called electrons. These move around the nucleus. It is an atom's electrons that are involved in reactions.

ELECTRON SHELLS

The electrons move in layers called shells that surround the nucleus. Larger atoms have more electrons than smaller ones. Their electrons are arranged in larger shells. Electrons fill the shells outward from the nucleus. The smallest shell is closest to the nucleus. The next shell is larger and contains more electrons; each new shell is farther from the nucleus and larger.

The electrons that reside in the outermost shell—the valence electrons—are the ones involved in chemical reactions. The number of an atom's valence electrons determines how that atom forms bonds with other atoms.

All metal atoms have only a few electrons in their outer electron shells. The atoms of a few metals have three or four outer electrons, but nearly all metal atoms have just one or two electrons. The low number of outer electrons makes metals behave and react in similar ways.

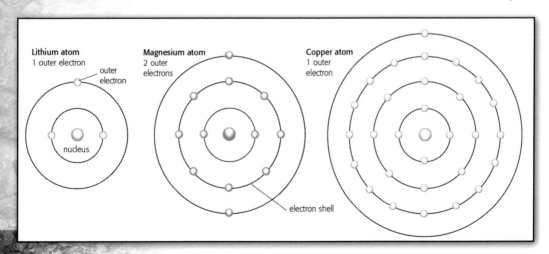

Lithium atom
1 outer electron
outer electron
nucleus

Magnesium atom
2 outer electrons

Copper atom
1 outer electron

electron shell

KEY DEFINITIONS

- **Atom:** The smallest unit of an element.
- **Bond:** An attraction between atoms.
- **Electron shell:** A layer of electrons that surrounds the nucleus of an atom.
- **Element:** The simplest type of substance made up of just one type of atom.
- **Nucleus:** The central core of an atom containing protons and neutrons.
- **Valence electrons:** The outermost electrons of an atom; they are involved in chemical reactions.

When an atom forms a bond, it gives, takes, or shares electrons in an effort to become stable. A stable atom is one where the outer shell is either full of electrons or empty. An atom with a nearly full outer shell will not give away its electrons easily. Instead, it will gain electrons from other atoms to become stable. An atom with only a few outer electrons will give them away easily. That makes its outer shell empty and the atom stable.

Nearly all metals have atoms with just one or two valence electrons. (A handful of metals have three or four.) So

HISTORY

GOLD AND GREED

The Inca people lived in the Andes Mountains of Peru from 1438 to 1533. They constructed great cities of stone buildings in the mountains. Inca buildings are all the more amazing because they were built without metal tools. Incas could not purify copper or iron. Instead, they used hard stones to make hammers, axes, and other equipment. However, Inca civilization used large amounts of another metal—gold. Inca people dug up pure gold, which they called the "sweat of the Sun." They used it to make cups, jewelry, and statues, but gold is too soft to make other tools. Gold was so common that it was not very valuable to the Incas. However, the first Europeans to come to Peru had different values.

Spanish explorers were the first to visit the Incas in 1532. The Incas presented their vistors with fine cloth, but the Spanish leader, Francisco Pizarro (circa 1475–1541), was more interested in their gold. After beating him in battle, Pizarro held Atahualpa, the Inca king, a prisoner until his people paid a huge ransom. The Incas filled one room with gold and two more with silver items, but

This painting shows the Inca hiding their reserves of gold.

Pizarro did not keep his side of the bargain and executed Atahualpa anyway.

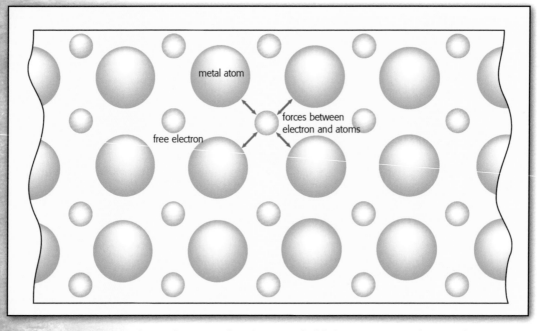

Free electrons surround metal atoms. The electrons hold the atoms together in what is known as metallic bonding.

metallic elements generally give away electrons to form bonds. This behavior is what makes metals all so similar.

FORMING BONDS

Metals are held together by metallic bonds. These bonds form when metal atoms share their outer electrons with each other. The outer electrons break off from the atoms and form a pool, or "sea," of electrons. The sea of electrons surrounds the metal atoms. Each free electron is attracted to the several nuclei around it. Because the particles are being pulled in all directions at once, the sea of electrons forms a "glue" that holds the metal atoms together.

The sea of electrons can flow through the metal. This ability gives metals many of their physical properties.

METALLIC PROPERTIES

As we have seen, metallic elements share similar atomic structures and they bond to each other in a certain way. As a result metals share many properties:

- **Solid and shiny:** Tightly packed metal atoms form a solid and are able to reflect light well, making the metal appear shiny.

- **Flexible:** The sea of electrons that binds metal atoms can flow around. The atoms are not held firmly in one place, so metals can be bent or hammered into a new shape without breaking.

• **Ductile:** As a metal is stretched into a wire, the sea of electrons continues to flow around the atoms. As a result, the metallic bonds can hold even thin wires together.

• **Conductive:** The sea of electrons is constantly moving. If the electrons are made to flow in one direction, they form an electric current.

• **High boiling and melting points:** Metallic bonds are strong bonds, so solid metals are generally tough solids. Strong bonds also require a lot of heat energy to break them so the solid can melt into a liquid, and even more to boil a liquid metal into a gas.

METALLIC REACTIONS

Metals are reactive elements because they readily give or share their valence (outer) electrons. Two common chemical reactions involving metals are combination and displacement reactions.

During these reactions metals become ions. An ion is an atom that has lost or gained one or more electrons. Metal atoms lose their outer electrons and form positively charged ions. Atoms

The Statue of Liberty in New York Harbor is made of copper. It was built in 1886, and, over the years, the copper has reacted with chemicals in the air to make a blue-green compound called verdigris.

that gain electrons from metals during a reaction become negatively charged ions.

Ions with opposite charges are attracted to each other. This attraction creates a bond between the ions and forms an ionic compound.

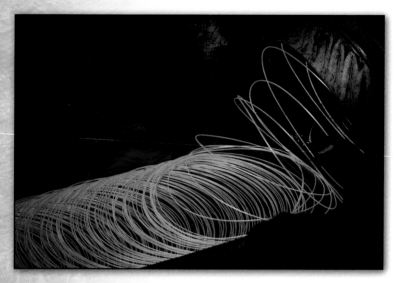

Coils being made from hot steel. When hot, the metal is soft enough to bend and mold into shape. When it cools down, the steel will be hard and very tough.

Most ionic compounds form when a metal gives electrons to a nonmetal. A common example of an ionic compound is potassium chloride (KCl). It is created when potassium (K) bonds with chlorine (Cl). With one valance electron to give away, potassium reacts easily. Chlorine is a nonmetal gas. Its atoms need one electron to become stable. Put potassium and chlorine together, and potassium atoms will lose their outer electrons and give them to the chlorine:

$$2K + Cl_2 \rightarrow 2KCl$$

MORE OR LESS REACTIVE

Some metals are more reactive than others. A reactive metal loses its outer electron or electrons more easily than a less reactive one. As a result, metal atoms are often involved in displacement reactions. These occur when a reactive element replaces a less active element in a compound. For example, potassium is more reactive than calcium (Ca). So pure potassium will react with calcium chloride ($CaCl_2$) to produce pure calcium and potassium chloride. However, pure calcium is not reactive enough to displace potassium from its compounds.

KEY DEFINITIONS

• **Compound:** A substance formed when atoms of two or more different elements bond together.

• **Conductive:** Describes a substance that carries electricity and heat well.

• **Ductile:** Describes a solid that can be drawn into long wires without breaking.

• **Malleable:** Describes a material that can be pounded into a flat sheet.

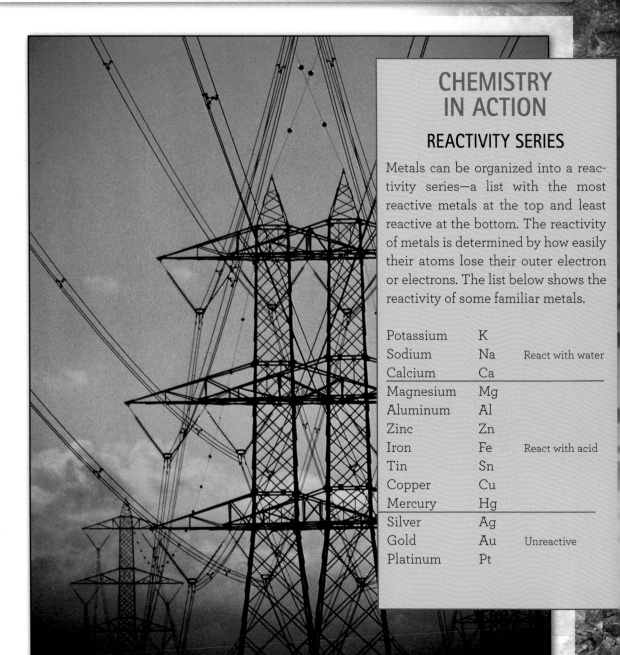

CHEMISTRY IN ACTION
REACTIVITY SERIES

Metals can be organized into a reactivity series—a list with the most reactive metals at the top and least reactive at the bottom. The reactivity of metals is determined by how easily their atoms lose their outer electron or electrons. The list below shows the reactivity of some familiar metals.

Potassium	K	
Sodium	Na	React with water
Calcium	Ca	
Magnesium	Mg	
Aluminum	Al	
Zinc	Zn	
Iron	Fe	React with acid
Tin	Sn	
Copper	Cu	
Mercury	Hg	
Silver	Ag	
Gold	Au	Unreactive
Platinum	Pt	

Metals are highly versatile. These pylons are made from steel, which makes them very strong structures. The steel is sometimes coated with a layer of zinc, another metal, to prevent it from rusting. The electricity wires strung between the towers are made of aluminum. This metal is a good conductor but is also very light.

CHAPTER TWO

THE HIGHLY REACTIVE ALKALI METALS

Alkali metals are the most reactive group of metals. The most common alkali metals are sodium and potassium. These metals are included in many useful compounds, such as table salt, baking powder, and gunpowder.

The elements in Group 1, the first column on the left of the periodic table, are known as the alkali metals. The group includes six metals—lithium (Li), sodium (Na), potassium (K), rubidium (Rb), cesium (Cs), and francium (Fr). The first five of these metals were discovered in the 19th century when scientists

Soap compounds contain the alkali metals sodium and potassium. The compounds form bubbles when mixed with water.

CHEMISTRY IN ACTION
ALKALI-METAL COMPOUNDS

Compound	Formula	Common name	Use
Sodium chloride	(NaCl)	Table salt	Used to flavor food
Sodium bicarbonate	$(NaHCO_3)$	Baking powder	Helps baked foods rise
Sodium hydroxide	(NaOH)	Lye	Used to make soap
Potassium carbonate	(K_2CO_3)	Potash	Used to make glass, enamel, and soap
Potassium chloride	(KCl)	—	Used as a plant fertilizer
Potassium nitrate	(KNO_3)	An ingredient	Used to make gunpowder and of saltpeter glass and to cure meat

A crop-dusting airplane sprays fertilizer on crops. Many plant fertilizers contain alkali-metal compounds.

figured out how to purify them from compounds found in nature. English chemist Humphry Davy (1778–1829) discovered potassium and sodium in 1807. Lithium was discovered by Swede Johann Arfvedson (1792–1841) in 1817. German Robert Bunsen (1811–1899) discovered cesium and rubidium in 1861. Francium was discovered in 1939, but it is the rarest element on Earth and very little is known about it.

Though each chemist used a different method to discover the elements, they realized the new metals had a similar atomic structure and shared many chemical and physical properties. For example, the alkali metals, known as such because many of their compounds are alkalis, are much softer than most other metals.

ONE OUTER ELECTRON

The alkali metals have only one valence electron in the outermost shell. As a result, they readily give away this electron to become more stable. Hydrogen also has one electron to give away and is sometimes included in Group 1. However, hydrogen is a gas in normal conditions and is not considered to be a metal.

It is their single outer electron that makes the alkali metals very reactive. A reactive element forms bonds with other atoms easily during chemical reactions.

ALKALIS: THE OPPOSITE OF ACIDS

Alkali metals are so called because they form compounds that are alkali. Alkalis are also referred to as bases. They are ionic compounds—made up of ions with opposite charges that are attracted to each other. Alkalis contain high numbers of negative hydroxide ions (OH-). An alkali's positive ion is generally a metal. For example, sodium hydroxide (NaOH) is made of a sodium ion (Na+) bonded to a hydroxide ion.

An acid is the opposite of an alkali. It has a high number of hydrogen ions (H+). When an alkali reacts with an acid, the hydroxide and hydrogen ions combine to produce water (H_2O). The other elements in the acid and alkali compounds also form a product, which chemists call a salt. For example, sodium hydroxide and hydrochloric acid (HCl) react to form water and sodium chloride (NaCl). Sodium chloride is table salt, which is used to flavor food. This reaction is written like this:

$$NaOH + HCl \rightarrow NaCl + H_2O$$

Chemists measure the number of ions in acids and alkalis using the pH scale. A pH lower than 7 is considered acidic, and a pH higher than 7 is considered alkaline. Water has a pH of 7 so is neutral—neither acid nor base.

THE PROPERTIES OF ALKALI METALS

Because all of the alkali metals have a similar atomic structure, they also look alike and behave in the same way. Alkali metals have the following physical and chemical properties:

- **Soft:** All the alkali metals are soft enough to be cut with a steel knife. As the size and mass of an alkali-metal atom goes up, the metal gets softer. So the farther down the column on the periodic table, the softer the metal. For example, cesium is almost liquid at room temperature. The softness is due to weak metallic bonds. Alkali-metal atoms have just one electron each to form the sea of electrons, and the electrons are spread thinly among the metal atoms. As a result, the bonds that hold the atoms together are not strong.

- **Shiny and silvery:** All the alkali metals are shiny. Most are silvery gray, although cesium has a golden tinge.

TAKING A CLOSER LOOK AT

PURIFYING ALKALI METALS

The alkali metals are very reactive. Although many of them are common in nature, they always occur combined with other elements to make compounds, such as table salt.

Chemists cannot extract alkali metals using chemical reactions and have to use electricity instead. An electric current separates the elements in certain compounds through a process called electrolysis. Even the most reactive elements, including alkali metals, can be separated in this way. However, more reactive elements require larger electric currents.

During electrolysis, positively and negatively charged rods are immersed in a liquid containing the compound to be split apart. Each rod attracts particles with an opposite charge, breaking the compound's bonds and separating the different ingredients.

This was the technique used by Humphry Davy in 1807 to purify first potassium and then sodium. That was the first time anyone had purified alkali metals. Davy used a simple battery called a pile to produce an electric current. Davy's assistant was Michael Faraday (1791–1867), who continued the study of electricity and later invented the electric motor.

- **Good conductors:** All the alkali metals conduct heat and electricity well.

- **Distinctive colors:** When the alkali metals are burned, they produce flames with characteristic colors. Lithium burns dark red, sodium is yellow, potassium is lilac, rubidium is also red, and cesium produces a blue flame.

- **Highly reactive:** The alkali metals are stored in oil, so they do not react with oxygen in the air. Some reactions are so fast and intense that they create an explosion of heat and gas. Alkali metals with large atoms are more reactive than the metals with small and light ones—large atoms lose their single outer electrons more easily during reactions.

KEY DEFINITIONS

- **Alkali:** A compound that contains large amounts of hydroxide (OH-) ions.

- **Chemical reaction:** A process in which atoms of different elements join or break apart.

- **Compound:** A substance formed when atoms of two or more different elements bond together.

- **Ion:** An atom that has lost or gained one or more electrons.

FORMING BONDS

The single outer electron of the alkali metals is the key to how their atoms behave with other elements. To become stable, an alkali-metal atom must lose its single outer electron to empty its outer shell. It does this by forming an ionic compound.

An ionic compound is produced when a metal atom gives an electron to a nonmetal atom. The atom that gives away an electron loses a negative charge and becomes a positive ion. Chemists call positively charged ions cations. The atom that takes an electron receives an extra negative charge and becomes a negatively charged ion. Chemists call that an anion. The opposite charges of the cation and anion attract each other, which results in an ionic bond forming between them, creating a compound.

Sodium chloride is created in this way from sodium (Na) and chlorine (Cl). Sodium is a typical alkali metal. It has one electron to give away before becoming stable. Chlorine is a nonmetal gas in need of one electron to fill its outer shell and become stable.

Put sodium and chlorine in a container together, and sodium will lose its electron (becoming the cation Na+) while chlorine takes the same electron (becoming the anion Cl-). The Na+ cation bonds with the Cl- to form the compound NaCl, the chemical formula for table salt. The reaction is written as:

$$2Na + Cl_2 \rightarrow 2NaCl$$

Alkali metals with large atoms are more reactive than those with smaller atoms. In a smaller atom such as lithium, the outer electron is nearer to the nucleus. As a result, the electron is held in place more strongly and is less likely to be involved in a chemical reaction. In a larger atom, such as one of potassium, the outer electron is held in place weakly and is more easily lost during a reaction.

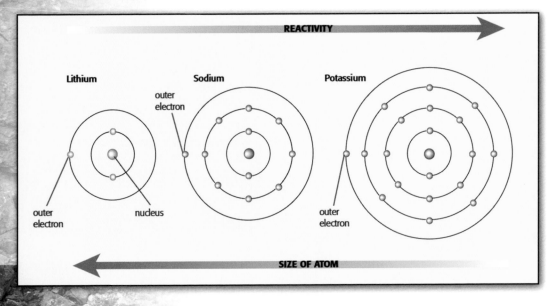

FORMING ALKALI COMPOUNDS

One of the most important reactions of alkali metals is with water. This is the reaction that produces the main alkali compounds for which the metals are named. In most cases, the reaction is violent, with the metal bursting into flames. Cesium reacts so explosively that it will shatter even a thick glass container.

As the least reactive alkali metal, lithium reacts with water more slowly. When you add lithium (Li) to water (H2O), the metal atom combines with an oxygen and hydrogen atom from the water. Together they become a lithium cation (Li+) and a hydroxide anion (OH-). These ions bond forming the alkali lithium hydroxide

(LiOH). The hydrogen atoms left over from the water form into pairs (H2). These hydrogen molecules are released as gas. The equation for this reaction is:

$$2Li + 2H_2O \rightarrow 2LiOH + H_2$$

SOURCES OF ALKALI METALS

Sodium and potassium are the two most important alkali metals; they are the sixth and seventh most abundant elements on the planet. Sodium and potassium salts are dissolved in seawater. Sodium makes up more than 1 percent of seawater. Potassium is less common.

Compounds of both metals are found in many types of minerals and rocks. The other alkali metals are quite rare. Francium is radioactive so its atoms break apart into other elements. Chemists estimate that there is only 1 ounce (28 g) of francium on Earth at a single point in time.

None of the alkali metals are found as pure elements in nature because they are so reactive. Instead they occur as salts. A salt is a compound formed when an acid reacts with an alkali.

Sodium's most common salt is sodium chloride (table salt). Others include saltpeter (sodium nitrate; $NaNO_3$), which is an ingredient of gunpowder and used to make glass, and borax (sodium borate; $Na_2B_4O_7$), which was once used in soaps.

Potassium chloride (KCl) is that metal's most common salt. Another one is potash (potassium carbonate; K_2CO_3). This is also called salt of tartar. Potash is used to make soft, luxury soaps.

Potassium reacts with oxygen in the air and burns with a bright lilac flame. Only potassium produces flames of this color.

TRY THIS

FIZZING ROCKET

The reactivity of alkali metals can be used to power a homemade rocket. You will need a toilet-paper roll, an empty film canister, a paper plate, some water, and half an indigestion tablet, such as Alka-Seltzer.

Tape the toilet-paper roll so it stands upright on the plate. Half fill the canister with water. Put the plate on the ground in an open space outside. Drop the half tablet into the canister and quickly close the lid, making sure it is on tight. Turn the canister upside down and drop it into the toilet-paper roll. Stand back and wait for several seconds. Caution: do not look down the toilet-paper roll.

Soon the canister will launch into the air. The water will spill out into the toilet-paper-roll launcher and plate, so you may need to replace them if you want to repeat the activity several times.

The canister rocket is powered by the reaction between the tablet and the water. The tablet contains sodium bicarbonate, which produces bubbles of carbon dioxide gas when it reacts with water. The gas builds up inside the canister. Eventually the pressure of the gas gets so high that it pushes off the canister's lid so it can escape. As the gas rushes out, it pushes the canister up through the launcher and high into the air.

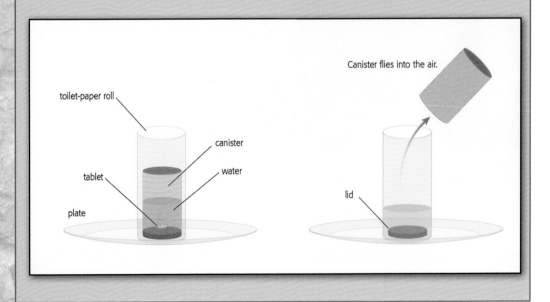

toilet-paper roll

canister

tablet

water

plate

Canister flies into the air.

lid

KEY DEFINITIONS

• **Electron shell:** A layer of electrons that surrounds the nucleus of an atom.

• **Ionic bond:** A bond produced when oppositely charged ions are attracted to each other.

• **Molecule:** Two or more atoms connected together.

• **Salt:** A compound made from positive and negative ions that forms when an alkali reacts with an acid

In most cases, the alkali metals are purified by electrolysis, a process that breaks salts apart using electricity. The electrolysis of sodium chloride produces sodium and chlorine atoms. The equation for this process looks like this:

$$2NaCl \rightarrow 2Na + Cl_2$$

PUTTING ALKALI METALS TO USE

The number of industrial uses for the alkali metals is huge. For example, the yellow streetlights you see along major roadways get their color from sodium gas glowing inside. Sodium bicarbonate ($NaHCO_3$), or baking powder, is used to make cakes. The compound reacts with water in the cake mix and releases carbon dioxide gas (CO_2). This gas is trapped as bubbles inside the cake, making it light and spongy.

Alloys of the alkali metals are also very useful. Sodium is used to purify titanium and mercury, while an alloy of sodium and potassium collects the heat produced in nuclear reactors.

The yellow light of these streetlights is produced by sodium gas. The gas gives out light when an electric current runs through it.

CHAPTER THREE

CALCIUM AND THE OTHER ALKALINE-EARTH METALS

The alkaline-earth metals are similar to the alkali metals but are harder and less reactive. This group's most familiar member is calcium. Calcium-containing compounds, such as limestone, occur in large amounts in nature.

The elements in the second column of the periodic table, called Group 2, are known as the alkaline-earth metals. These six elements—beryllium (Be), magnesium (Mg), calcium (Ca), strontium (Sr), barium (Ba), and radium (Ra)—were not purified until the 19th century. However, many of their compounds had been known about since much earlier times. For example calcium-containing compounds, such as marble, a type of calcium carbonate ($CaCO_3$), has been used as a building material for thousands or years. As early as the first century BCE, the Romans were making buildings from concrete that contained quicklime (calcium oxide; CaO).

Seashells are made of calcium carbonate, a compound that contains an alkaline-earth metal.

CHEMISTRY IN ACTION

ALKALINE-EARTH-METAL COMPOUNDS

Compound	Formula	Common name	Use
Calcium oxide	CaO	Quicklime	Used in building materials
Calcium carbonate	$CaCO_3$	Limestone, calcite	Used in mortar and toothpaste
Calcium sulfate	$CaSO_4$	Gypsum	A fertilizer and fireproofing agent
Magnesium carbonate	$MgCO_3$	Magnesite	Gymnastic chalk
Magnesium hydroxide	$Mg(OH)_2$	Milk of magnesia	Indigestion remedy
Magnesium silicate	$MgSi_4O_{10}$	Soapstone	Talcum powder
Magnesium sulfate	$MgSO_4$	Epsom salts	Laxative

Alkaline-earth metals are named for these and other compounds. *Earth* is an old name for a naturally occurring compound. Before the study of chemicals became scientific in the 17th century, people thought different earths were elements themselves. They noticed that some of the earths were similar to the alkaline substances such as lye (sodium hydroxide; $NaOH$). They were called alkaline earths. Once it was found that these substances were really compounds containing metals, the metals were named the alkaline-earth metals.

Calcium and magnesium, the two most common alkaline-earth metals, were discovered by English chemist Humphry Davy (1778–1829). He made this discovery in 1807, a year after isolating some of the first alkali metals.

The last member of the group to be discovered was radium, which was isolated by Marie (1867–1934) and Pierre Curie (1859–1906) in 1898. Radium is radioactive, so particles break away from its atoms' nuclei. This changes the number of particles in the atom, so

KEY DEFINITIONS

- **Compound:** A substance formed when atoms of two or more different elements bond together.

- **Nucleus:** Central core of an atom.

- **Radioactive:** When an atom has an unstable nucleus that breaks apart.

it becomes an atom of another element. The particles given out by radioactive elements are termed radiation.

TWO OUTER ELECTRONS

The atoms of alkaline-earth metals have two electrons in their outer shell. These are the valence electrons, which take part in chemical reactions.

To become stable, the atoms must give away or share these two electrons. In most cases, the alkaline-earth metals readily give away the two electrons, making them reactive metals.

THE PROPERTIES OF ALKALINE-EARTH METALS

The alkaline-earth metals all have two valence electrons and so have similar properties. Their properties resemble those of the alkali metals, but their behavior is less extreme. Alkaline-earth metals have the following properties:

- **Soft:** They are harder than the alkali metals but still softer and more malleable (flexible) than most other metals.

- **Good conductors:** All of them conduct heat and electricity well.

- **Distinctive colors:** All these metals burn with bright white flames, but when heated they produce light with a certain color. For example, calcium produces dark red flame, strontium a brighter red, and barium produces green flames.

- **Reactive:** Alkaline-earth metals are very reactive but less so than alkali metals. The alkaline-earth metals hold onto their two outer electrons more tightly than the alkali metals hold their one outer electron. The metals become more reactive going down the group.

CHEMISTRY IN ACTION
HARD WATER

Water that contains the alkaline-earth metals calcium or magnesium is commonly called hard water. The alkaline-earth metals dissolved in hard water react with soap and stop it from forming bubbles.

Hard water comes from deep underground, where it trickles through rocks containing calcium and magnesium compounds.

Removing the metals "softens" the water. Hard water also tastes different from soft water because it contains more minerals.

Hard water produces limescale when it is heated. This chalky substance blocks pipes and coats

A heating element is coated in limescale from hard water. A layer of limescale stops the element from heating water efficiently.

heating elements in kettles and washing machines. Softening the water removes the scale.

- **Shiny:** Pure alkaline-earth metals are silver colored and shiny. However, the more reactive members of the group, such as strontium and barium, soon become dull gray. That is because the metals react with oxygen in the air and are covered in a layer of metal oxide.

SOURCES OF ALKALINE-EARTH METALS

Calcium and magnesium are the two most common alkaline-earth metals. Calcium makes up about 3 percent of Earth's rocks. It is the third most abundant element on the planet. Magnesium makes up about 2 percent of the Earth's rocks and is the eighth most abundant element on the planet. The other alkaline-earth metals are rare. None of the alkaline-earth metals are found as pure elements in nature because they are so reactive.

Calcium occurs mostly in soils as calcium carbonate, an ingredient in limestone. Magnesite, or magnesium carbonate ($MgCO_3$), is one of the most common natural magnesium compounds.

Alkaline-earth metals are purified by electrolysis. This is a process in which a powerful electric current is used to split a compound into its elements. Calcium chloride ($CaCl_2$) and magnesium chloride ($MgCl_2$) are used for this process. As well as pure metal, the reaction also produces chlorine gas (Cl_2):

$$CaCl_2 \rightarrow Ca + Cl_2$$

FORMING BONDS

Most alkaline-earth metal compounds are ionic. Ionic compounds are formed when one atom loses electrons and another gains them. An alkaline-earth metal atom forms an ion by losing its two outer electrons. This results in an ion with a charge of 2+, which is written as, for example, Ca^{2+}. The lost electrons are picked up by the atoms of another element. Those atoms become negatively charged ions. Ions with opposite charges are attracted to each other and they bond into a compound.

Pure alkaline-earth metals will react with oxygen (O) in the air to form an ionic compound called an oxide. For example, magnesia (magnesium oxide; MgO) is made up of one magnesium ion (Mg^{2+}) bonded to an oxide ion ($O2-$). The two electrons given away by the magnesium have been picked up by the oxygen. The equation for this chemical reaction is:

$$2Mg + O_2 \rightarrow 2MgO$$

KEY DEFINITIONS

- **Acid:** A compound that contains large amounts of hydrogen (H+) ions.

- **Alkali:** A compound that contains large amounts of hydroxide (OH-) ions.

- **Atom:** The smallest piece of an element that retains the properties of the element.

- **Bond:** An attraction between atoms.

- **Ion:** An atom that has lost or gained one or more electrons.

Cascades of calcium carbonate at Pamukkale in Turkey. These formations are produced by spring water that contains a lot of dissolved calcium minerals.

CHEMICAL REACTIONS OF ALKALINE-EARTH METALS

Calcium carbonate ($CaCO_3$) from limestone has many uses. For example, it is used in the production of steel.

TRY THIS

TESTING ALKALIS AND ACIDS

Alkaline-earth metals make compounds that are alkaline. You can investigate how they react with an acid using this activity. You will need lemon juice, some milk of magnesia (an indigestion medicine), and indicator paper. Lemon juice is an acid, which contains many hydrogen ions. It turns indicator paper red. Milk of magnesia is magnesium hydroxide, $Mg(OH)_2$, an alkali. It contains many hydroxide ions and turns indicator paper blue.

Begin by testing the juice with a piece of indicator paper. Put the paper on one side to dry so you can compare its color with later tests. Add three tablespoons of milk of magnesia to the juice and stir the mixture. Re-test the liquid with a strip of indicator paper. Compare the color of this strip. It should be less red than the first. This is because the milk of magnesia and some of the acid ions have reacted to produce neutral products.

Keep adding more magnesia and re-testing the mixture. The mixture will gradually lose its acidity and become alkaline. At this point, the paper will turn dark green.

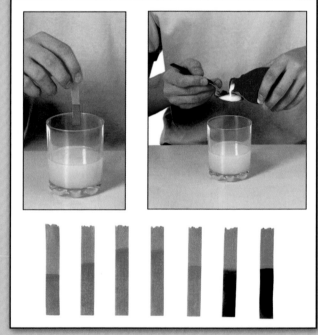

Lemon juice is acidic, but as more and more milk of magnesia is added to the lemon juice, the mixture becomes increasingly alkaline. Testing with indicator paper shows a gradual change from red to dark green.

However, limestone is also turned into a quicklime (CaO) through a simple reaction. When limestone is heated, it decomposes into quicklime and carbon dioxide gas (CO_2):

$$CaCO_3 \rightarrow CaO + CO_2$$

Quicklime is a reactive substance. It is an ingredient in plaster, mortar, and cement. When water (H_2O) is added to quicklime, a reaction takes place that is known as slaking. The reaction produces slaked lime or calcium hydroxide—$Ca(OH)_2$:

$$CaO + H_2O \rightarrow Ca(OH)_2$$

Slaked lime is an alkali—a substance that contains a lot of hydroxide ions (OH-). Alkalis react with acids, which are compounds that contain a lot of hydrogen ions (H+).

When quicklime is added to mortar or another building material, it is mixed with water. The two compounds react,

CHEMISTRY IN ACTION

BODY WORKS

Calcium is the most common alkaline-earth metal found in the human body. Two percent of an adult's weight is made up of calcium. Most calcium is in the teeth and bones, in the form of calcium phosphate and calcium carbonate. These compounds make bones and teeth hard.

Water in the human body, such as in the blood and inside cells, contains dissolved calcium ions. The calcium ions are involved in making muscles move and in sending electricity around the brain and along nerves.

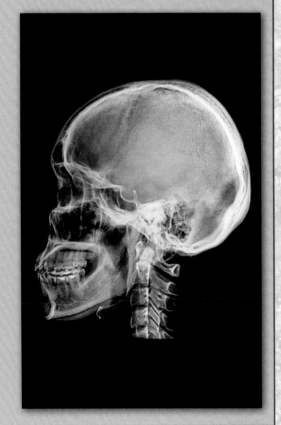

An X-ray of a person's head shows the hard skull and teeth, which contain calcium compounds.

A gymnast uses a powder on his hands to help him grip. The powder is magnesium carbonate. It is often called "chalk," but it is not the same as the substance used on blackboards.

and the resulting slaked lime then undergoes another reaction. Carbon dioxide in the air dissolves in water inside the mortar to make a carbonic acid (H_2CO_3). This acid reacts with the slaked lime to form calcium carbonate and water. The reaction looks likes this:

Water cascades from holes along the front of the Grand Coulee Dam on the Columbia River.

TOOLS AND TECHNIQUES
WRITING ON THE WALL

Teachers use a common calcium compound in the classroom. The chalk used to write on blackboards is a type of limestone, which contains calcium carbonate. Chalk forms from the remains of tiny sea organisms. When they die, their shells, which contain calcium carbonate, build up in piles in shallow waters. Over the years the shells form a thick layer and are squeezed into chalk.

$$Ca(OH)_2 + H_2CO_3 \rightarrow CaCO_3 + 2H_2O$$

Calcium carbonate occurs naturally in limestone, and, following these reactions, the mortar has literally turned to stone.

PUTTING ALKALINE-EARTH METALS TO USE

Alkaline-earth metals have many other uses. Magnesium is alloyed with aluminum to make strong but light objects, such as aircraft. Beryllium is added to copper to make it harder.

Until about 1950, radium was used to make paints that glowed in the dark. The glow came from the radioactive atoms releasing radiation. We now know that radiation of this kind can be harmful to humans. Today radium is only used in safe ways.

CHAPTER FOUR

ALUMINUM AND THE OTHER GROUP 13 METALS

Aluminum, the most abundant metal in Earth's rocks, belongs to Group 13 of the periodic table. This group's other members are much rarer.

The elements in the 13th column of the periodic table, called Group 13, include the metals aluminum (Al), gallium (Ga), indium (In), and thallium (Tl). Aluminum is the most important and most abundant metal in this group. The group also includes boron, which is a metalloid.

Crushed aluminum cans waiting to be recycled. This metal is recycled because pure aluminum is very expensive to make.

CHEMISTRY IN ACTION

GROUP 13 COMPOUNDS

Compound	Formula	Common name	Use
Aluminum chlorohydrate	$Al_2(OH)_5Cl$	—	Used in deodorants
Aluminum oxide	Al_2O_3	Alumina; corundum	Found in rubies and sapphires
Gallium arsenide	GaAs	—	Produces laser light
Indium phosphide	InP	—	Used in semiconductors
Thallium bromide	TlBr	—	Used in heat detectors
Thallium sulfate	Tl_2SO_4	—	Rat and ant poison

Aluminum-containing compounds were used by the ancient Greeks and Chinese. Roman doctors also used them to slow bleeding from cuts. They called the compounds alums, and that is where we get the name *aluminum*. The metal was first purified in 1825 by Danish chemist Hans Christian Oersted (1777–1851).

Gallium, indium, and thallium were all discovered in the mid-19th century using spectroscopes, instruments that read the unique light pattern produced when materials are heated.

THREE OUTER ELECTRONS

All Group 13 metals have three valence electrons in their outer electron shells. To become stable, atoms must give or share these three electrons. Losing three electrons requires a lot more energy than losing one or two. As a result, Group 13 metals are only mildly reactive, much less so than alkali metals, for example.

THE PROPERTIES OF GROUP 13 METALS

Aluminum, gallium, indium, and thallium have many of the classic metal properties. They are all gray or silver in color and shiny. They also conduct heat and electricity very well. However, it is their soft and flexible nature that makes these metals unusual.

Aluminum is the second most malleable (moldable) metal on Earth (second only to gold). Gallium, indium, and thallium are very soft. Each has an unusually low melting point and is nearly liquid in normal conditions.

Large passenger aircraft, such as this Boeing 747, are made from aluminum alloys. Aluminum is strong but also very light, making large aircraft light enough to fly.

THE SOURCES OF GROUP 13 METALS

Aluminum is the most abundant metal in Earth's crust, making up about 7 percent of rocks and minerals. Yet it is one of the most difficult metals on the planet to make in a pure form.

Like most metals, aluminum does not appear in nature as a free element. The main aluminum ore is alumina (aluminum oxide; Al_2O_3). Pure alumina is a colorless and extremely stable compound that takes a lot of energy to split into individual elements. The compound is known also as corundum. It is the main substance in ruby and sapphire gemstones.

Aluminum has only been produced in large amounts for about 100 years. It is purified through a complex process that involves both electrolysis and smelting. Today, many aluminum objects are made from recycled metal. It takes 20 times less energy to reuse aluminum than it does to purify it.

Gallium, indium, and thallium are rare and found mostly in the ores of other metals, such as copper, zinc, and lead. They are extracted as by-products when these other metals are refined.

FORMING BONDS

The three valence electrons in the outer shells of Group 13 metals are key to how they react with other elements. To become stable, an atom of one of these metals must give away its three electrons to empty its shell.

Most metals bond ionically, but the Group 13 elements can also form covalent bonds. An ionic bond is one that forms when ions with opposite charges attract each other. The atoms of Group 13 metals form ions by losing three outer electrons to become, for example, Al^{3+}. These ions are attracted to negatively charged ions, which have gained electrons.

A covalent bond forms when atoms share pairs of electrons instead of giving away or gaining them. By sharing, each atom can fill its outer shell with electrons and become more stable. A few Group 13

HISTORY

MAKING PURE ALUMINUM

Charles Martin Hall (1863–1914) was a U.S. chemist who invented an inexpensive way of making pure aluminum. Hall made his discovery in 1886, aged just 23. He did his research in a laboratory in his house in Oberlin, Ohio.

The process became known as the Hall-Héroult process because Frenchman Paul Héroult (1863–1914) developed a similar system at the same time. Before the Hall-Héroult process was invented, pure aluminum was as expensive as silver. Although aluminum compounds were common, it was very difficult to refine the metal.

Hall's discovery changed all that and made it possible for aluminum to be used in all kinds of ways. The Hall-Héroult process is still used today. It involves electrolysis, in which an electric current splits alumina (aluminium oxide; Al_2O_3) into pure aluminium and oxygen. This is done at a high temperature, so the alumina is melted into a liquid.

Charles Martin Hall invented an inexpensive method for making pure aluminum.

KEY DEFINITIONS

- **Covalent bond:** A bond in which atoms share electrons.

- **Ionic bond:** A bond produced when oppositely charged ions are attracted to each other.

- **Malleable:** Describes a material that can be bent easily or pounded into a flat sheet.

- **Molecule:** Two or more atoms connected together.

- **Metalloid:** A substance with the properties of both a metal and a nonmetal.

- **Ore:** A mineral that contains valuable amounts of a metal.

- **Refine:** To purify a metal by removing unwanted elements.

compounds, such as aluminum iodide (AlI_3), are covalent. However, most Group 13 metals form ionic compounds.

Alumina (Al_2O_3) is a typical example of an ionic compound. It forms when aluminum comes in contact with the oxygen (O_2) in the air. The equation for the chemical reaction is:

$$4Al + 3O_2 \rightarrow 2Al_2O_3$$

In each molecule of alumina, two Al^{3+} ions are bonded to three O^{2-} ions.

Alumina forms as a thin layer on the surface of the metal. That stops oxygen from getting to the pure metal underneath, so the reaction cannot continue.

Gallium, indium, and thallium are all more reactive than aluminum. As the metal with the largest atoms, thallium is the most reactive. It must be stored underwater to prevent it from reacting with oxygen in the air.

THE CHEMICAL REACTIONS OF GROUP 13 METALS

Aluminum is often used as a reducing agent. A reducing agent is a compound that gives away electrons during a chemical reaction. Aluminum is the reducing agent for an important reaction called the thermite process. This reaction is used to make pure iron from iron oxide (Fe_2O_3). The aluminum atoms give electrons to the iron ions (Fe^{3+}) during the reaction. As a result the aluminum atoms become ions (Al^{3+}) and bond to the oxide ion (O^{2-}) to form alumina. The Fe^{3+} ions become atoms of pure iron. The reaction looks like this:

$$Fe_2O_3 + 2Al \rightarrow Al_2O_3 + 2Fe$$

Common chemical reactions of gallium, indium, and thallium are harder to describe, partly because they are rare. Gallium can corrode other metals—a chemical reaction in which one metal oxidizes another.

PUTTING GROUP 13 METALS TO USE

Aluminum is one of the most useful metals on Earth. Not since iron replaced bronze as the most useful metal at the dawn of the Iron Age has a metal been

Gallium's melting point is 86°F (30°C). The heat from a hand is enough to turn gallium into a liquid.

TOOLS AND TECHNIQUES

STUDYING LIGHT

Many rare metal elements were discovered using a tool called a spectroscope. Spectroscopes use a triangular lens called a prism to split light into different colors. When it is heated or burned, each element produces light containing a unique set of colors. When light from a flame is split into colors by a spectroscope, chemists can see what elements are involved in the reaction. Some of the Group 13 metals produce interesting colors. For example, indium is named for the bright indigo color seen in the light it emits.

more important. Although iron is still the most-used metal, aluminum's properties make it useful in different ways. For example, it is light and so is used to make aircraft and electricity cables that are hung from pylons. It is also malleable and can be molded into many shapes. Perhaps the most common shape is that of an aluminum can.

Most aluminum products are alloys (mixtures of metals). Small amounts of copper, zinc, magnesium, and silicon are added to it to make it harder.

Alumina is used to protect steel (an iron alloy) from rusting. A thin layer of the compound is coated on the steel. The coating stops oxygen and moisture from getting to the iron underneath.

White light contains all the colors of the rainbow. A prism separates these colors.

CHAPTER FIVE

TIN, LEAD, AND THE OTHER GROUP 14 ELEMENTS

Model soldier made of an alloy of tin and lead. The alloy is easy to melt and pour into molds.

Tin and lead are familiar metals because they have been used by people for many thousands of years. Both are easy to purify and are unreactive and so are often used to protect other metals from damage.

The metals tin (Sn) and lead (Pb) appear in the 14th column of the periodic table, which is known as Group 14. Tin and lead are the only metals in this group. The other Group 14 elements are germanium and silicon, which are classed as metalloids, and carbon, which is a nonmetal.

People have used tin and lead for 7,000 years. Tin was added to copper to make the alloy bronze. Lead was bent into tubes and other useful shapes.

No one knows who first discovered and named these metals. Their chemical symbols come from their Latin names—*stannum* for tin, and *plumbum* for lead.

It is easy to make pure tin and lead. Rocks sometimes contain pure lead. However, neither of the metals is very common in nature.

FOUR OUTER ELECTRONS

The atoms of tin and lead each have four valence electrons in their outer shell. To become stable, these atoms need eight or no electrons in their outer shells. That can be achieved by losing four electrons or gaining four. Both options require a lot of energy. As a result, tin and lead are not very reactive elements, and they are not involved in many chemical reactions with other elements.

While the four valence electrons make tin and lead fairly unreactive, they also enable the atoms to form very stable bonds. A stable bond is one that is not easily broken. Once a tin or lead atom bonds with another element, that bond is very hard to break.

Tin and lead are described as "poor metals" because they do not react in the same way as other metals. The only

Small rings of molded tin. When it is cold, tin is easy to bend but becomes more likely to break when it is heated. Most metals are easier to bend when warm.

metals that are less reactive than tin and lead are the so-called precious metals, such as gold and platinum.

THE PROPERTIES OF TIN AND LEAD

The atomic structure of tin and lead helps create an important characteristic of both elements—the ability to resist corrosion. Corrosion is a chemical reaction between a metal and its environment, usually the oxygen and water in the air, which weakens the metal. Rusting is a type of corrosion.

Tin and lead do not rust because they react only slowly with oxygen to form oxides. Like other lead and tin

KEY DEFINITIONS

• **Alloy:** A metallic substance that contains two or more metallic elements.

• **Electron shell:** A layer of electrons that surrounds the nucleus of an atom.

• **Valence electrons:** The outermost electrons of an atom, which are involved in chemical reactions.

CHEMISTRY IN ACTION

COMPOUNDS AND ALLOYS OF TIN AND LEAD

Compound/Alloy	Formula	Common name	Use
Lead acetate	$Pb(C_2H_3O_2)_2$	Sugar of lead	A poisonous, sugarlike substance used in dyes and varnish
Lead carbonate	$2PbCO_3$	White lead	A white pigment (coloring)
Lead oxide	PbO	Litharge	Once used to make yellow paint and glass
Lead tetraoxide	Pb_3O_4	Red lead	A red pigment
Niobium-tin	Nb_3Sn	—	A superconductor that conducts electricity very well
Bronze	60% Cu, 40% Sn	—	An alloy containing tin (Sn) and copper (Cu)
Pewter	85% Sn, 15% Pb	—	A substitute for silver once used to make shiny objects
Solder	60% Sn, 40% Pb	—	An alloy used to fuse metals
Tin tetrachloride	$SnCl_4$	Stannic chloride	Used to toughen glass

A microchip is soldered into place. The solder is an alloy of tin and lead. It is melted by a hot soldering iron. The melted alloy flows around the chip. The solder cools and becomes solid again, holding the chip in place.

compounds, the oxides are very stable. They form a thin layer on the surface of the metals. This layer acts as a barrier between the air and the metal, which prevents any more reactions from taking place.

Tin and lead also share other properties. Both are soft metals that can be bent or molded easily. They have low melting and boiling points compared to other metals. Both are also poor conductors of electricity and heat compared to other metals.

THE SOURCES OF TIN AND LEAD

Both tin and lead occur only in very small quantities in Earth's crust. If you took a random scoop of one million pieces, or parts, of the Earth's crust, only two parts would be tin and twelve parts would be

A CLOSER LOOK

LEAD POISONING

People have used lead for many thousands of years, but only recently did we learn that lead can damage the human nervous system and cause blood and brain disorders.

Today, lead has been removed from paints, gasoline, and ceramics to protect people from its harmful effects. However, lead was a common cause of illness in the past. For example, lead is thought to have made many Romans insane. They used lead water pipes and even added lead to their food as a sweetener.

German composer Ludwig van Beethoven (1770–1827) may have also been poisoned by lead. Lead could have gotten into his body through eating fish and drinking wines sweetened with lead, and using pewter dishes. Beethoven was also often ill with stomach problems. When he died, doctors found that his organs were damaged in a way that might have been caused by lead.

Caligula (12–41 CE) was an insane Roman emperor. He made his horse the leader of his government. The emperor's mental illness may have been a result of lead poisoning.

lead. Scientists call this way of measuring parts per million, or ppm. In this case, the Earth's crust is 2 ppm tin and 12 ppm lead.

Tin occurs as ores—minerals that contain a useful amount of the metal. Much of the world's tin is contained in the mineral cassiterite, which is mainly tin oxide (SnO_2). Cassiterite tends to be located in soft ground close to the surface. As a result, it is mined using the open-pit method. Some mines have tunnels leading down to the ore. However, an open-pit mine is just a huge hole dug into the ground. The largest tin mines are in Malaysia.

Lead is sometimes found as a pure metal, especially near volcanoes where the heat causes minerals to react. Most lead is found in the form of the mineral galena (lead sulfide; PbS). Galena and other lead ores are generally located deep underground in hard rocks.

The metal is also found in the ores of other metals, such as silver and copper.

THE CHEMICAL REACTIONS OF TIN AND LEAD

Having four valence electrons makes tin and lead unreactive metals. To form a bond with another atom, the tin or lead atom must give away its four outer electrons and become an ion. An ion is an atom that has lost or gained electrons and has become charged as a result.

Tin and lead atoms form ions with a charge of 4+. Losing four electrons

Galena is the most common lead-containing compound in nature.

requires a lot of energy, which is why tin and lead do not react easily.

Ions are attracted to other ions with an opposite charge. This attraction forms bonds between the ions and creates an ionic compound. For example, tin ions (Sn^{4+}) bond to two oxide ions (O^{2-}) to form cassiterite (SnO_2). Galena (PbS) is one lead ion (Pb^{4+}) bonded to one sulfide ion (S^{4-}).

Pure tin and lead are removed from their compounds by reacting them with carbon (C). This is a displacement reaction in which the carbon takes the place of the metal in the compound. The reaction requires heat, which is supplied by burning the carbon. (Coal is a fuel made of mainly carbon.) For example, tin is extracted from cassiterite, in a chemical reaction that looks like this:

$$SnO_2 + 2C \rightarrow 2CO + Sn$$

CHEMISTRY IN ACTION
CAN MAN

French inventor Nicolas François Appert (1750–1841) invented a way of keeping food fresh by storing it in airtight containers. He invented this process in 1809 for the French emperor Napoleon Bonaparte. Napoleon wanted a way for his army to carry food without it going bad. Appert put raw food in glass jars sealed with corks. He then boiled the jars until the food inside was cooked. This process killed all the bacteria that could rot the food. In 1811, a British company started to use metal cans instead of jars. The cans did not break as easily. The metal used was iron coated in a layer of tin to stop it from rusting—the tin can was born.

KEY DEFINITIONS

- **Compound:** A substance formed when atoms of two or more different elements bond together.

- **Conductor:** A substance that carries electricity and heat well.

- **Ion:** An atom that has lost or gained an electron or electrons.

- **Mineral:** A naturally occurring compound, such as those that make up rocks and soil.

- **Ore:** A mineral that contains valuable amounts of a metal.

PUTTING TIN AND LEAD TO USE

Tin and lead have many uses. Tin is used to protect other metals from rusting. Food cans are coated with a layer of tin for this reason. They are still referred to as tin cans in some parts of the world, although most of the metal in them is steel (a strong alloy of iron containing carbon and other elements).

Tin is also a common ingredient in alloys. Bronze, pewter, and solder all contain large proportions of tin. Pewter and solder also contain lead.

Lead is used a lot less than tin because it is poisonous. However, it is used to make ammunition, glass, ceramics, brass, and

Gasoline used to have lead compounds in it to help it burn evenly. However, the lead came out in the exhaust fumes and damaged people's health. Today, most gasoline is unleaded.

cable covers. As a very heavy metal, lead is used in weights. More than half of the lead used today comes from recycled products.

CHAPTER SIX

SILVER, GOLD, AND THE OTHER TRANSITION METALS

Nearly half of all metals are transition elements. These metals form a block across the center of the periodic table. Many of the most common and familiar metals, such as copper, iron, and gold, are transition metals.

The elements between the third and twelfth columns of the periodic table are called the transition series. This block contains about 30 elements, all of which are metals.

The transition metals include some metals that have been known about for

Many gemstones are colored by transition metals. Chromium makes emeralds green and rubies red, while titanium makes sapphires blue.

thousands of years, such as iron (Fe), silver (Ag), and copper (Cu). The other metals in the series have been discovered over the past 300 years. Transition metals with lower atomic numbers, and therefore with smaller and lighter atoms, were generally discovered before the elements with larger, heavy atoms. Heavy metals tend to be more reactive than lighter ones, thus they are more difficult to isolate from compounds.

Widely used transition metals include manganese (Mn), chromium (Cr), cobalt (Co), nickel (Ni), tungsten (W), and titanium (Ti). The rarer transition metals include molybdenum (Mo), palladium (Pd), rhodium (Rh), and zirconium (Zr).

THE VARYING ATOMIC STRUCTURE OF TRANSITION METALS

The transition metals form a series rather than a group. That is because they all share an unusual atomic structure that separates them from all other metals. However, they also have a varying number of outer electrons, so they cannot be formed into a group in the same way as other metals. Nevertheless, like most of the other groups of metals, transition metals have just one or two electrons in their outermost electron shells. These electrons are valence electrons and so are involved in chemical reactions with other elements.

Some of the largest human-made objects in the world, such as this tanker, are made from steel—an alloy containing mainly iron.

With one or two outer electrons, transition elements react in the same way as alkali metals and alkaline-earth metals. The transition metals are generally less reactive than these other groups. We find the reason for this by looking more closely at the elements' atomic structures. As well as in the outer electron shell, transition elements also have valence electrons in the next shell in toward the nucleus.

CHEMISTRY IN ACTION

TRANSITION-METAL COMPOUNDS

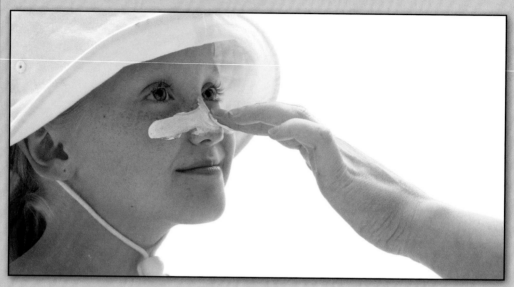

Many sun-protection creams contain zinc oxide, a white substance that blocks ultraviolet light. Ultraviolet (UV) light is invisible radiation that is produced by the Sun. UV radiation can damage the skin causing sunburn and tanning. Zinc oxide is used to make space suits UV-proof. It is also used to make white paints and inks.

Compound	Formula	Common name	Use
Brass	67% Cu, 33% Zn	—	Alloy used to make ornaments and musical instruments
Cobalt oxide	CoO	Cobalt blue	A deep blue compound used to color glass and china
Copper sulfate	$CuSO_4$	—	Used as a pesticide
Hematite	Fe_2O_3	Black diamond	The main iron ore
Lead chromate	$PbCrO_4$	Chrome yellow	A bright yellow pigment
Manganese dioxide	MnO_2	Pyrolusite	Used in batteries
Stainless steel	90% Fe, 10% Cr	—	Used to make shiny objects that do not rust
Vanadium pentoxide	V_2O_5	—	A catalyst used to produce sulfuric acid

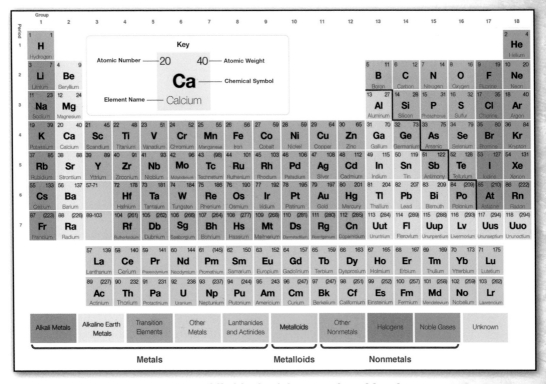

The transition metals form the middle block of the periodic table. The term *transition*, which means "to change from one thing to another," is used because the block connects the two sides of the table.

FILLING ELECTRON SHELLS

An atom's electrons are arranged in shells that fit inside one another. The smallest and innermost shell contains just two electrons. The second shell is larger and can hold up to eight electrons. The third shell is larger still and has room for up to 18 electrons. However, instead of filling up with this number of electrons, once the third shell has eight electrons, it stops accepting any more. The fourth shell then begins to fill up. The story does not end there. Once the fourth shell has

KEY DEFINITIONS

- **Alloy:** A metallic substance that contains two or more metallic elements.
- **Electron shell:** A layer of electrons that surrounds the nucleus of an atom.
- **Metal:** A substance that is solid, shiny, moldable, and that can carry electricity.
- **Ore:** A naturally occurring substance that contains valuable amounts of a metal.
- **Valence electron:** One of the outer electrons in an atom that is involved in chemical reactions.

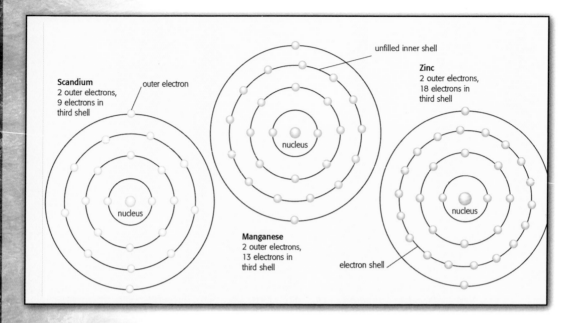

Scandium
2 outer electrons,
9 electrons in
third shell

outer electron

nucleus

Manganese
2 outer electrons,
13 electrons in
third shell

nucleus

unfilled inner shell

Zinc
2 outer electrons,
18 electrons in
third shell

nucleus

electron shell

two electrons, the third shell begins to accept electrons again.

GAINING ELECTRONS

To illustrate this, let us compare the atomic structures of calcium and scandium. Calcium is the last element in the periodic table before the transition series begins. Scandium is the first member of the series. Calcium atoms have four shells. The third shell has eight electrons, and the fourth has two. Scandium atoms also have four shells. As in calcium, the fourth shell has two electrons, but the third shell has nine.

The third shell continues to fill up producing a series of metal atoms with

A piece of zinc. Zinc is one of the most reactive of the transition metals.

Like most metals, the transition metals have one or two outer electrons. However, the next shell in can have anything from 8 to 18 electrons. These inner electrons also take part in reactions.

four electron shells. Most of these atoms have two outer electrons, although a few such as chromium and copper have one.

The third shell is finally full in the atoms of zinc, where it contains 18

electrons. At this point, the fourth and outer shell begins to fill up again.

Following zinc, atoms of the metal gallium form. Gallium is not a transition metal. Its atoms have a third shell with 18 electrons, and a fourth shell with three electrons.

The fourth shell continues to gain electrons until it holds eight in the atoms of the gas krypton. As happened with the third shell, the fourth shell now stops accepting any more electrons. A fifth electron shell begins to form. Once this shell holds two electrons, the fourth shell beneath it then continues to fill. Another

series of metal atoms with five shells and one or two outer electrons is formed. The same process also occurs in atoms with six shells. The transition series ends with mercury (Hg).

THE PROPERTIES OF TRANSITION METALS

Transition metals tend to be good conductors, and they are the toughest metals, with much higher melting points than the metals in other groups. However, there are some notable exceptions. For example, mercury is liquid at room temperature, and gold is very malleable.

Many of the elements' properties are the result of how their atoms bond

A bridge made of steel, an alloy of iron and carbon with other metals mixed in. Steel is extremely strong but can also be molded and bent.

Mercury is the only metal that is liquid in normal conditions. Its chemical symbol is Hg. That comes from the Latin word *hydrargyrum*, which means "water silver."

together. In most cases, the transition metals have a lot of valence electrons. As well as being involved in reactions, these also help form metallic bonds. The more electrons metal atoms use to form these bonds, the stronger they will be. Having strong bonds between its atoms makes a metal very hard. The strong bonds hold each atom in a fixed position, and it takes a large force to break them apart or push them into a different shape. However, many hard transition metals, such as iron and chromium, are also brittle. That is, when they do break they shatter into pieces. These metals are made less brittle by being alloyed with other substances.

The strong bonds also make the metal atoms pack tightly together, and, as a result, some transition metals are very dense. Measuring a substance's density is

An assortment of batteries. Batteries contain transition metals such as nickel, cadmium, and manganese. They are involved in reactions that produce electric currents.

TOOLS AND TECHNIQUES
MEASURING TEMPERATURE

We take advantage of mercury being a liquid at everyday temperatures in a tool used to measure temperature: the thermometer. This instrument was invented in 1592. It is a hollow glass tube marked with the temperature and filled with mercury. As it gets warm, the mercury expands and moves up the glass tube, indicating a change in temperature. Today, mercury thermometers are only used under controlled conditions because the metal is extremely poisonous.

This mercury thermometer is designed to measure a day's maximum and minimum temperatures.

a way of comparing how big it is (volume) with how heavy it is (weight).

A handful of a dense substance weighs more than the same volume of a less dense substance. The densest element of all is the transition metal osmium (Os). A cube of this metal with sides measuring 1 inch (25 mm) weighs a surprising 13 ounces (22.5 g/cm³). That is 22.5 times heavier than the same volume of water.

The strong bonds also result in high melting and boiling points because it takes a lot of energy to break the bonds. Most transition metals melt at temperatures above 1,832°F (1,000°C). Tungsten has the highest melting point of any metal: 6,192°F (3,422°C).

THE SOURCES OF TRANSITION METALS

A few transition metals, such as mercury, gold, and platinum, are found pure in nature. Others occur in minerals combined with other elements. Useful metals, such as iron and copper, are extracted from such minerals, which are called ores. Ores are minerals that contain large amounts of a valuable metal. Other transition metals are rare and are not refined from their own ores. Instead, they are produced as by-products when more common metals are being produced.

Iron is the planet's most common element. Scientists think that Earth's core is a huge ball of hot iron and nickel (another transition metal). However, only about 5 percent of the Earth's crust is iron, making it the fourth most abundant element in rocks. Most iron occurs bonded to oxygen to make compounds called iron oxides.

KEY DEFINITIONS

• **By-product:** A substance that is produced when another material is made.

• **Earth's crust:** The layer of solid rock that covers the surface of Earth.

• **Melting point:** The temperature at which a solid substance melts into a liquid.

• **Mineral:** A natural compound, such as those that make up rocks and soil.

The other transition metals that are mined for their ores are nickel, zinc, and titanium. Of these transition metals, titanium is the ninth most abundant and

A vast pit created by digging copper ore from the ground.

A crystal of hematite. This mineral is a compound containing iron and oxygen. Hematite is the main ore of iron.

zinc is the 23rd most abundant element in Earth's crust. Nickel and copper are not far behind.

The ores are generally found near the surface, so they are dug up directly from the surface, creating huge holes or pits in the process.

The ores of iron and other transition metals are refined to make pure metals

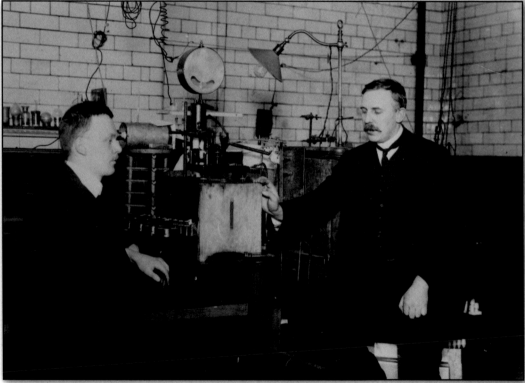

Transition metals with atomic numbers 104 to 112 are artificial elements made in laboratories. They are made by chemists fusing smaller atoms. These metals are named for famous scientists. Rutherfordium, for example, is named for Ernest Rutherford, the New Zealand chemist who discovered the atomic nucleus. Rutherford is seen here on the right, photographed in 1908.

using a process called smelting. In this process metal oxides are reacted with carbon (C). During the reaction, the carbon takes oxygen out of the ore, leaving pure metal behind.

Rarer transition metals are purified in the same way, generally as by-products. For example, rhodium is a by-product of nickel production, and cadmium is a by-product of zinc refining.

GIVING, TAKING, AND SHARING VALENCE ELECTRONS

The atomic structure of transition metals has a great effect on how these elements form bonds with other elements. Atoms bond to each other by giving, taking, or sharing their valence electrons. The atoms do this to fill or empty their outer electron shells.

The transition metals have valence electrons in two electron shells rather than just the outer one like most other elements. So the way their atoms use these electrons to form bonds with other atoms is far more complicated.

Most of the nontransition elements must lose, gain, or share a fixed number of electrons in order to become stable and form a bond. However, transition metals can form compounds by using a varying number of their valence electrons. That makes the chemical behavior of transition metals so complex. In many cases, an atom of a transition metal can form three or four different compounds with atoms of another element.

CALCULATING LOST AND GAINED ELECTRONS

Chemists figure out how a transition element forms its bonds by calculating

There are four types of cobalt ions, each one with a certain oxidation state. The oxidation number goes up each time the cobalt loses an electron.

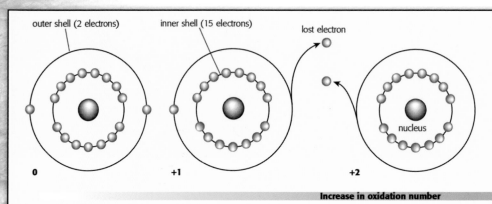

outer shell (2 electrons) inner shell (15 electrons) lost electron

nucleus

0   +1   +2

Increase in oxidation number

something called the oxidation state. Despite its name, the oxidation state is just a number that tells chemists how many electrons an atom has lost or gained as it formed a compound with other elements. For example, when the nontransition metal magnesium (Mg) reacts with the nonmetal oxygen (O_2), it loses its two valence electrons. As a result it forms an ion with a charge of 2+ (Mg^{2+}). An ion is an atom that has lost or gained an electron and so has become charged. The oxygen gains two electrons to fill its outer shell and forms the negatively charged ion O^{2-}. In this example, the magnesium has an oxidation state of +2, while the oxygen has a state of -2.

Most transition metals can have more than one oxidation state. For example, those of manganese are +7, +4, +3, and +2. In other words, manganese atoms can lose up to seven electrons during a reaction. That is more than any other metal. Iron has the oxidation states of +3 and +2, while copper's are +2 and +1.

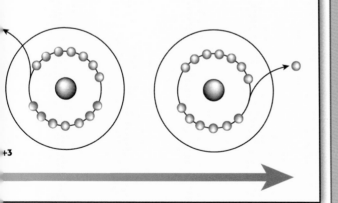

+3

TOOLS AND TECHNIQUES
PURIFYING METALS

Many metals are purified from their ores by a process called smelting. Iron is the main metal to be smelted, but manganese, cobalt, and nickel are also purified in this way.

Smelting is a series of chemical reactions in which the ore reacts with carbon (C) and then carbon monoxide (CO). The products of the reactions are pure metal, carbon dioxide (CO_2), and waste, known as slag. The reaction's chemical equation looks like this:

$$2Fe_2O_3 + 3C \rightarrow 4Fe + 3CO_2$$

Evidence of iron smelting dates back thousands of years but no one knows who discovered the technique. Today, iron smelting takes place in a chimney-shaped blast furnace. Iron ore is heated with coke, a type of coal that is almost pure carbon. The ore melts and reacts with the carbon to produce carbon monoxide. This gas also reacts and removes the last of the oxygen from the ore to produce pure molten (melted) iron and carbon dioxide. Oxygen is also blasted through the mixture to burn away impurities.

A few transition metals have just one oxidation state. For example, scandium's is +3, and zinc only forms ions with a oxidation state of +2.

FORMING COMPOUNDS

The oxidation state of a transition metal tells chemists how many ions are needed to make a compound. Like most other metals, transition metals make ionic compounds. These are produced when ions bond together. Ions are attracted to other ions with an opposite charge. This attraction is what creates a bond between the two ions.

While the ions that make up a compound are charged, the compound itself is neutral—it does not have a charge. That is because the opposite charges of the ions balance each other. So the oxidation state, or charge, of a transition-metal ion determines how many ions it bonds with.

For example, when copper has an oxidation state of +1 (Cu+) it takes two ions to form a compound with an oxygen ion (O^{2-}). The compound has the formula Cu_2O. Chemists call this compound cuprous oxide, or copper (I) oxide—the "I" is "one" in Roman numbers. When copper has an oxidation

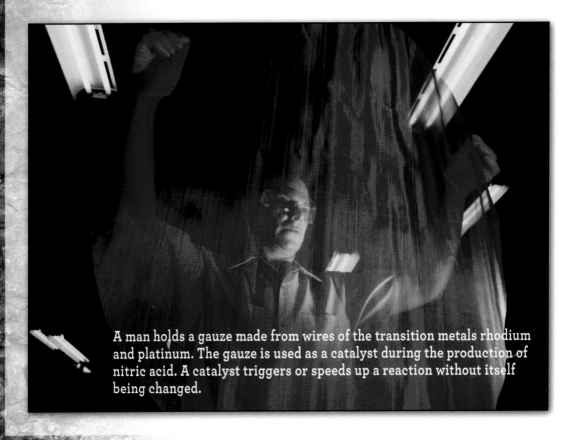

A man holds a gauze made from wires of the transition metals rhodium and platinum. The gauze is used as a catalyst during the production of nitric acid. A catalyst triggers or speeds up a reaction without itself being changed.

CHEMISTRY IN ACTION
METALS IN THE BLOOD

Iron is vital in blood because it bonds with oxygen. The iron is part of a large molecule called hemoglobin. This molecule makes our blood red. Hemoglobin picks up oxygen molecules that are breathed into the lungs and then carries them throughout the body. However, not all animals use iron for this purpose. The king crab, which is an ocean-living relative of scorpions and spiders, uses copper compounds instead of iron ones to transport oxygen around in its body. The crab's blood is blue owing to the copper.

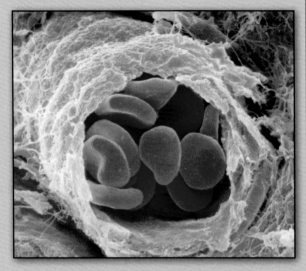

A magnified image of blood cells traveling through a blood vessel. The cells are red because they contain a lot of hemoglobin.

state of +2 (Cu^{2+}), it forms cupric oxide—copper (II) oxide (CuO).

CATALYSTS

The transition metals are often good catalysts. A catalyst is something that makes a chemical reaction go faster. One example, known as the Haber process, uses iron (Fe) to make ammonia (NH_3). The chemical reaction looks like this:

$$N_2 + 3H_2 \xrightarrow{\text{Fe}} 2NH_3$$

Putting its symbol above the arrow shows that the iron is the catalyst and not a reactant or product. The iron plays a part in the reaction but is not used up by it. In this example, the iron catalyst gives and takes electrons (changing its oxidation state), so the nitrogen (N) and hydrogen (H) atoms have more chances to bond with each other.

Another reason transition metals are good catalysts is because other substances can stick to their surfaces. While the substances are stuck, atoms can rearrange to form new chemical substances. One chemical reaction that uses a transition-metal catalyst in this way converts small organic (carbon-based) chain molecules into larger ones. For example, ethane (C_2H_4) reacts with hydrogen (H_2) to become propane (C_3H_6) when heated in the presence of a nickel catalyst.

A metal catalyst that works in this way adsorbs the other atoms. Notice that this word does not have the same meaning as absorb. When something is *absorbed* it becomes mixed into another substance. When it is *adsorbed*, a substance clings to the surface of another, but remains separate.

PUTTING TRANSITION METALS TO USE

Transition metals are the metals used in industry

These rings are made from platinum. Platinum is a precious metal, along with gold and silver. These transition metals do not react very easily, so they do not rust or tarnish quickly and stay shiny and clean for long periods. They are described as precious because they are rare metals and therefore expensive.

to make everything from rust-proof roofs to earrings. However, many of the metals are also important for the chemical reactions that take place inside living bodies. Without tiny amounts of several transition metals in their bodies, people would become ill.

As we have seen, an iron compound is used in our blood to transport oxygen. It also makes blood red. Human bodies use other transition metals in similar ways. Several are ingredients of vitamins. Cobalt, for example, is a vital part of vitamin B12, which occurs naturally in meat, eggs, and dairy products.

KEY DEFINITIONS

• **Catalyst:** An element or compound that helps a chemical reaction occur more quickly but that is not altered by the reaction.

• **Ion:** An atom that has lost or gained one or more electrons.

• **Ionic bond:** A bond produced between oppositely charged ions.

• **Oxidation state:** A number used to describe how many electrons an **atom** has lost or gained.

Shiny taillights on a car from the 1950s. This metal fitting is made from chrome, which is steel coated in a layer of chromium. The chromium protects the steel from rusting, keeping the metal shiny and reflective.

A close-up of a crystal of vitamin B12. This compound contains cobalt. B12 is also called cobalamin and is essential for good health. People who do not have enough vitamin B12 have problems with their blood.

TRY THIS

IRON IN FOOD

Many foods have iron added to them to make them healthful. You can extract the iron from breakfast cereal. You will need some cereal flakes, a Ziploc bag, a cup of water, plastic food wrap, a paper towel, and a small magnet taped to a wooden stick. Seal some flakes in the bag and crush them into a fine powder. Pour the powder into a bowl and mix it with the water. Stir the mixture of cereal for 10 minutes with the magnet covered in plastic food wrap. Wipe the food wrap with a paper towel. You should see tiny specks of black powder on the towel—the iron in your cereal. Repeat with other cereals and compare the amount of iron you find.

The body also needs minute amounts of chromium, manganese, copper, zinc, and several other transition elements to stay healthy. However, if people eat large amounts of these metals they will become ill.

In industry, iron is the most important of all metals. It is easy to find and inexpensive to refine. About 95 percent of all the pure metal produced each year is iron. In its pure form, iron is very brittle and not very useful. However, when it is alloyed with a small amount of carbon, it becomes a flexible and strong alloy called steel.

Many of the other transition metals are rarely used in their pure form. Instead, they are mixed with iron to

A five-cent coin, or nickel, is made from an alloy of nickel and copper. The coin was introduced in 1866 as an alternative to coins made of silver.

make steels with different properties. For example, chromium is added to make stainless steel, which does not rust. Steel containing molybdenum is very hard. Steel with a coating of zinc is called galvanized steel. This alloy is also rust-proof and is often used outdoors.

Transition metals that are used on their own include gold, silver, and titanium, which is both stronger and lighter than steel. Copper is a good conductor and is used to make electric wires. Zinc, cadmium, and nickel are used in batteries.

MAGNETIC TRANSITION METALS

Three transition metals—iron, cobalt, and nickel—can be made into magnets.

A magnet is an object that has two poles, known as north and south. When two magnets come together, the like poles repel each other, while opposite poles attract. The magnetic force that does this is produced by the electrons spinning inside the atoms of these three metals. No other elements, metal or nonmetal, can be used to make magnets.

An electromagnet picks up scrap iron at a junkyard. Electromagnets are magnets that can be turned on and off. They only work when an electric current runs through them.

CHAPTER SEVEN

THE MOST UNUSUAL METALLOIDS

The metalloids are the most unusual of all elements. They have properties of both metals and nonmetals. Many metalloids are semiconductors, which are substances used in electronics, such as computers and cell phones.

The metalloids, also known as the semimetals, are elements that have both metal and nonmetal properties.

These six elements—boron (B), silicon (Si), germanium (Ge), arsenic (As), antimony (Sb), and tellurium (Te)—form a jagged diagonal line separating the metals from the nonmetals on the periodic table. Polonium (Po), a radioactive element, is also sometimes considered a metalloid.

Arsenic and antimony have been used for thousands of years. Arsenic was commonly used as a poison and to make glass. Ancient Egyptians used poisonous antimony compounds in eye makeup. The other metalloids were discovered from the late 18th through the 19th century.

A circuit board with microchips and other electronics that contain metalloids, such as silicon and arsenic.

CHEMISTRY IN ACTION
METALLOID COMPOUNDS

Compound	Formula	Common name	Use
Antimony trioxide	Sb_2O_3	—	A fireproofing agent
Silicon dioxide	SiO_2	Silica or sand	Used to make glass and concrete
Sodium borate	$Na_2B_4O_7$	Borax	A component of soaps, cleaners, and bleach
Sodium silicate	Na_4SiO_5	Silica gel	A drying agent
Gallium arsenide	GaAs	—	Used in solar cells and lasers
Germanium tetrahydride	GeH_4	Germane	Used to make semiconductors
Cadmium zinc telluride	CdZnTe	—	An alloy used in radiation detectors and to make holograms
Lead arsenate	$PbHAsO_4$	—	An insecticide

The metalloids blend metallic and nonmetallic properties. Some are hard and slightly shiny; others are crumbly powders. A few conduct electric currents while others block them. In addition, unlike metals, metalloids are brittle and shatter easily.

THE ATOMIC STRUCTURE OF METALLOIDS

The metalloids belong to several groups in the periodic table—from column 13 to column 16. As a result, metalloids have a variety of atomic structures.

Boron has three electrons in its outermost shell; silicon and germanium have four outer electrons; arsenic and antimony have five outer electrons;

A technician holds a gallium arsenide semiconducting wafer containing thousands of chips for radio frequency communications devices.

tellurium and polonium have six valence electrons. These different atomic structures influence the properties of the metalloids considerably.

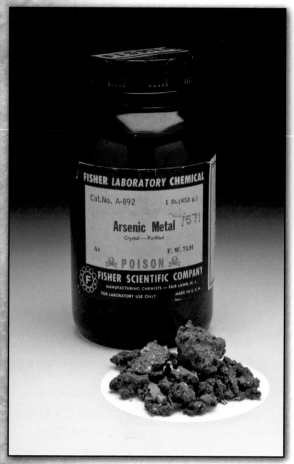

Pure arsenic takes two forms. Yellow arsenic is a powder that looks like a nonmetal. Gray arsenic is shiny and looks more like a metal.

KEY DEFINITIONS

• **Metal:** A hard but flexible element. Metals are good conductors. Their atoms have only a few outer electrons.

• **Metalloid:** An element that has both metallic and nonmetallic properties.

• **Nonmetal:** An element that is not a metal or metalloid. Nonmetals are poor conductors. Their atoms tend to have several outer electrons.

THE PROPERTIES OF METALLOIDS

As a result of their varying atomic structures, there are no properties shared by all metalloids. Instead, some metalloids are more metallic than others, while some are more nonmetallic. For example, pure germanium and polonium look more like metals than other metalloids, while boron and arsenic are more nonmetallic. Most metalloids exist in two forms when pure—one metallic, the other nonmetallic.

Metalloid	Appearance	Conductivity
Boron	Metallic and nonmetallic forms	Insulator
Silicon	Metallic and nonmetallic forms	Semiconductor
Germanium	Metallic	Semiconductor
Arsenic	Metallic and nonmetallic forms	Semiconductor
Antimony	Metallic	Semiconductor
Tellurium	Nonmetallic	Insulator
Polonium	Metallic	Insulator

A man who has been poisoned by arsenic in his well water. The arsenic has covered his hands with lesions.

THE SOURCES OF METALLOIDS

Silicon is perhaps the most important metalloid. It is the second most abundant element in Earth's crust. (Oxygen is the most common element.) Silicon makes up more than a quarter of Earth's rocks and minerals.

Silicon is never found uncombined in nature. Its most common compound is with oxygen—silicon dioxide (SiO_2). This substance is commonly called silica, and it is perhaps most familiar as the tiny crystals that make up sand. Silica also occurs in other forms, which go by other names. Quartz is a form of silica that is found in many rocks, such as granite. Flint is another form of the compound found in rocks. Many precious stones are colored forms of silica, including jasper, opal, agate, and onyx.

Although silicon compounds are very easy to find, the other metalloids are not. They almost always occur bound to other elements. In many cases, the metalloids are produced as by-products when refining other metals.

Arsenic commonly occurs as arsenopyrite (FeAsS), a compound of iron (Fe), arsenic (As), and sulfur (S). Because arsenic is poisonous and has few uses, it is not usually extracted from this ore. Instead, arsenic is a by-product in the treatment of other metals.

Boron has two main sources, the minerals borax and kernite. Both are forms of sodium borate ($Na_2B_4O_7$). The largest deposits of these minerals are underneath Boron, California, a town named for the metalloid.

Minerals containing the other metalloids do not exist in large amounts. Antimony occurs as a sulfide mineral called stibnite (SbS_3). However, stibnite

is rarely used to refine pure antimony. Antimony is made mainly as a by-product of silver and lead production. Tellurium is a common impurity in gold, lead, and

A crystal of quartz, which is a natural form of silica. Quartz is one of the most common minerals in rocks. Sand is made up of tiny grains of quartz.

A piece of gallium arsenide, a compound of the metal gallium and arsenic. This material is used to make very fast-working microchips. Microchips are made in clean, dust-free conditions. This person is wearing a suit and mask so he does not add impurities.

copper. Germanium is also a by-product of refining these metals and also zinc. Radioactive polonium is produced when radium breaks down . Polonium itself decays into lead.

FORMING BONDS

All the metalloids except boron have four or more valence electrons in their outermost shell. Because they need eight electrons to become stable, the metalloids most often get the extra outer electrons to fill their shells by sharing them with other atoms. This sharing forms covalent bonds.

Silica (SiO_2), the most common metalloid-containing compound, is held together by covalent bonds. The reaction that produces silica looks like this:

$$Si + O_2 \rightarrow SiO_2$$

However, the way atoms bond to form silica is more complicated than this equation shows. An oxygen atom has to share two electrons with other atoms to become stable. A silicon atom has four electrons to share. In silica each oxygen atom gets its two electrons from two silicon atoms and is bonded to both of them. Although its

CHEMISTRY IN ACTION
METALLOID COMPOUNDS

Silicon Valley is an area of northern California. Many of the world's microchips are made there. The area is so called because silicon is the most common material used in microchips. Silicon and some other metalloids are semiconductors. They conduct electricity only in certain conditions. This property makes them very useful for making electronic devices, such as transistors and diodes, which are used in computers and other machines. Transistors are switches that direct current around a circuit. Diodes are devices that allow current to travel in just one direction. Microchips contain tiny transistors, diodes, and other electronics.

A model of the first transistor from 1947.

formula is SiO_2, each silicon atom is bonded to four oxygens. Silica's bonds connect all the atoms in a vast network, or lattice. That makes it a very hard and stable compound.

PUTTING METALLOIDS TO USE

The most important use of metalloids is in semiconductors. Silicon and germanium are the main semiconducting metalloids. Other metalloids, such as arsenic, are added to semiconductors in tiny amounts to adjust their properties. This process is called doping.

Semiconductors are substances that conduct electricity in the presence of energy such as heat, light, or electrical energy. For example, thermistors

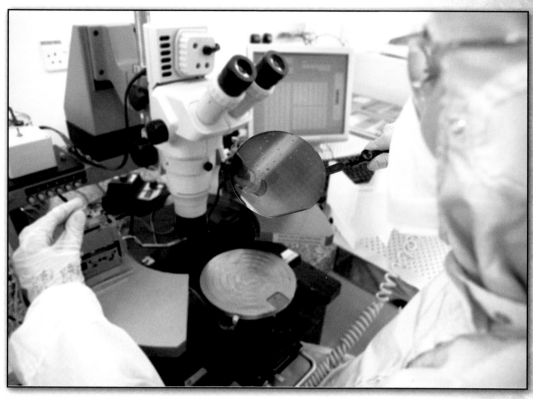

A thin wafer of silicon with electronic components etched on its surface. The wafer will be cut up into chips.

KEY DEFINITIONS

- **Covalent bond:** A bond in which two or more atoms share electrons.

- **Semiconductor:** A substance that conducts only in certain conditions

are semiconductors influenced by heat. They are used in thermometers and thermostats. Light-sensitive semiconductors are used in solar cells, which generate electricity from sunlight, and photoreceptors, which detect light. Digital cameras take pictures by recording the image formed on photoreceptors behind the lens.

Computers and similar machines are controlled by semiconductors that are influenced by electric currents. These devices act as switches and mechanisms that work together in large numbers to carry out complex tasks.

CHAPTER EIGHT

BIOGRAPHY: MICHAEL FARADAY 1791-1867

Michael Faraday came from a humble background, which perhaps makes his achievements in science all the more remarkable. His father, a blacksmith, suffered poor health and was often unable to work, so the family was poor. Faraday later said that his education consisted of "little more than the rudiments of reading, writing, and arithmetic." When he was 13, Faraday was sent as an apprentice to George Riebau, a London bookseller and book binder; this meant that Faraday would be taught Riebau's trade. Faraday made up for his lack of formal schooling by educating himself, partly by reading many of the books he was asked to bind. He was especially interested in books on science, and longed for the chance to pursue a scientific career.

As his interest in the subject grew, Faraday began to attend evening lectures at the City Philosophical Society. This was a self-improvement society, founded by a local group of young working men. Such societies were often

A portrait of English physicist and chemist Michael Faraday, most famous for his pioneering contributions to the fields of electromagnetism and electrochemistry.

attended by traveling lecturers who, for a small fee, would give short courses on popular scientific topics. Faraday taught himself enough about electricity to be able to address his fellow students on the subject.

A FRIEND IN HIGH PLACES

A turning point came in 1812 when one of Riebau's customers, knowing of Faraday's interest in science, gave him tickets to a series of lectures at the Royal Institution. The Royal Institution had been founded in 1799 by the American-born scientist Benjamin Thompson, later Count Rumford (1753–1814), with the aim of sharing scientific information or, as he put it, "diffusing the knowledge and facilitating the general introduction of useful mechanical invention and improvements." It regularly held lectures; the series that Faraday attended was given by one of the greatest scientists of the time, the chemist Sir Humphry Davy (1778–1829). Like Faraday, Davy had a keen interest in electricity as well as chemistry, and he was a popular speaker. Fascinated by his lectures, Faraday took detailed notes as Davy talked, then bound them as a book. A little while after, Davy had an accident; he needed a temporary assistant, and Faraday was recommended to him. While working with Davy he showed him the lecture notes he had collected. In 1813, a permanent job of laboratory assistant at the Royal Institution arose. Davy remembered Faraday and offered him the job.

The following year Faraday accompanied Davy on an 18-month tour of

Faraday at work in his basement laboratory, c. 1852.

KEY DATES

1791	Born on September 22 at Newington, Surrey, near London
1804	Apprenticed as a bookbinder
1812	Appointed laboratory assistant to Humphry Davy at the Royal Institution, London
1813	Accompanies Davy on European tour
1821	Establishes existence of electromagnetic rotation. Marries Sarah Barnard
1825	Appointed director of the Royal Institution laboratory
1827	Begins children's Christmas lectures at the Royal Institution
1831	Demonstrates electromagnetic induction
1833	Establishes two laws of electrolysis
1867	Dies at Hampton Court, Surrey, on August 25

continental Europe. Davy introduced him to several leading European scientists, among them French physicist André Ampère (1775–1836) and Italian physicist Alessandro Volta (1745–1827). Both men would later make important discoveries in the field of electromagnetism and have electrical units (the ampère, or amp, and the volt) named for them. Back in London, Faraday began his research as a chemist. In 1825, he became director of the laboratory at the Royal Institution and was made professor of chemistry in 1833. By then, he had begun his experiments in electricity.

EARLY ADVANCES IN THE STUDY OF ELECTRICITY

The word "electricity" comes from the Greek word "electron," which means amber. Amber is resin from trees that has become solid; when amber is rubbed vigorously, it becomes charged with "static" electricity. The ancient Greeks

Dutch physicist Peter van Musschenbroek's Leiden jar. The jar is charged using a wheel-operated generator. If a metal discharging rod is held near the jar, a spark jumps from the ball at the top, taking the charge down to the outer metal coating of the jar.

knew of this tendency. Because static electricity could attract things, people thought that magnetism and electricity might be related in some way but were not sure how.

The first major advance in the study of electricity came in 1746 when the Dutch physicist Peter van Musschenbroek (1692–1761), working in Leiden in the Netherlands, invented what became known as the Leiden jar. This consisted of a glass jar coated inside and out with metal. A chain ran from the lid into the jar; when the lid was linked to a friction machine, an electric charge passed down through the chain into the closed jar. The electric charge then passed into the metal coating and was stored. This type of storage device is now known as a capacitor. People found that if they touched the jar when it was charged, they would receive quite a shock; it became a popular source of party tricks. Musschenbroek himself swore that he would not be prepared to undergo a second shock even if he were crowned king of France.

American statesman Benjamin Franklin (1706–1790) was also intrigued by electricity. He carried out many experiments to determine its nature. Electricity was known to attract and repel, and it was Franklin who devised the term "positive" for its attractive force and "negative" for its repulsive force. His discovery that lightning is an electric charge led him to suggest a practical way of protecting buildings by proposing that metal rods, or lightning conductors, should be attached to the sides of buildings to draw the electric charge from a lightning strike and guide it safely down to the earth.

THE VOLTAIC PILE

The next major step in investigating electricity came in 1800, when Alessandro Volta built a "voltaic pile," or battery. The battery consisted of plates of metal, alternately zinc and silver, with a pad soaked in salt water between. A thin

The Voltaic pile uses three types of disks—zinc, silver, and a wet pad—that are stacked alternately. A chemical reaction between the disks causes an electric charge to flow along a copper wire running from the top silver disk to the bottom zinc disk.

An artist's depiction of Benjamin Franklin's famous experiment to prove that lightning and electricity are the same. He flew a kite in a thunderstorm and found that the wet string conducted electricity from the storm to charge a capacitor.

copper wire ran from the top disk to the bottom. A chemical reaction between the metals caused a small flow of electricity to run through the wire until the chemical energy of the disks, or the "cell," was exhausted. Unlike the charge in a Leiden jar, the battery created a continuous flow of electrical charge, which was called a "current."

Volta's work was quickly picked up by other scientists. Six weeks after he reported his findings, two English chemists, William Nicholson (1753– 1815) and Anthony Carlisle (1768–1840), found that the battery could be used to split water into its two parts: hydrogen and oxygen. When two metal plates, attached to the positive and negative sides of the battery, were suspended in water, bubbles of gas appeared. The two scientists collected the gas that gathered above the plates in test tubes and found that hydrogen gas collected at one plate and oxygen at the other. This process became known as electrolysis.

Davy used this to break down other oxides (an oxide is a compound of oxygen with another element). Within a few years, he had used the battery to separate from their oxides the previously unknown substances of chlorine, sodium, calcium, strontium, potassium, barium, and magnesium.

DISCOVERING

The first suggestion that there was a connection between magnetism and electricity came through the work of Danish physicist Hans Christian Oersted (1777–1851). In an 1820 experiment, he passed an electric current through a wire, which was pointing in a north–south direction. A compass happened to be lying beneath the wire, with its needle aligned in the same direction. As the current passed through the wire Oersted was astonished to see that the needle turned in a clockwise direction for a full 90 degrees so that it was at right angles to the wire. When he placed the compass above the

This is a replica of the original electrolysis trough made in 1810 by James Powell, adopting techniques pioneered by Humphry Davy. Electrolysis is a technique in which electric current is passed through solutions or molten materials. This method can separate compounds into their elements by supplying or removing electrons from the outer shell of their atoms.

wire, the needle deviated 90 degrees in the opposite direction. Oersted realized that the magnetic effect of the electricity was moving the needle. This is known as electromagnetism.

BUILDING A DYNAMO

In 1821, following reports of Oersted's experiments, Faraday decided to see if he could make a wire rotate continuously by electromagnetism. His successful experiment is shown on page 76. In creating electromagnetic rotation, Faraday had converted electrical movement into mechanical movement, and in doing so, had invented the first electric motor.

Over the next 10 years, Faraday continued his chemistry work while pursuing his growing interest in electricity. His next big breakthrough in electromagnetism came in 1831, when he created the apparatus that allowed him to find "electrical induction." Unknown to him, American physicist Joseph Henry (1797–1878) had independently carried out similar experiments a year before, but Faraday published his results first and is better remembered for the discovery.

Oersted shows colleagues how electricity flowing along a wire deflects a compass.

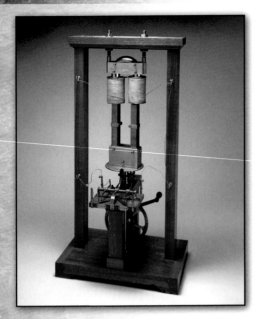

An electromagnetic machine (*left*) built in 1832 by French scientist Hippolyte Pixii (1808–1835), based on Faraday's description of electromagnetic induction. The machine used the motion between a rotating magnet and stationary induction coils to generate electricity. Faraday created bursts of "induced" current; these were the first dynamos, converting mechanical energy into electrical energy. Dynamos are used nowadays in many different ways, from powering automobile batteries to producing a public electricity supply.

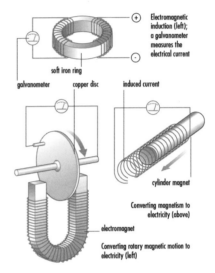

Electromagnetic induction (left); a galvanometer measures the electrical current

soft iron ring

galvanometer   copper disc   induced current

cylinder magnet

Converting magnetism to electricity (above)

electromagnet

Converting rotary magnetic motion to electricity (left)

Faraday wound a coil of insulated wire connected to a battery around one side of an iron ring. He wound a second coil of wire around the opposite side of the ring and ran the wires to a galvanometer, a sensitive instrument for measuring electrical currents. When he switched the current on, it flowed through the first wire. This magnetized the iron ring and caused a brief current, recorded on the galvanometer, to flow through the second coil. The same thing happened when the current was switched off because current only flows when a magnetic field varies or moves (by being switched on or off, for instance).

Faraday called these bursts of current "induced." He was able to produce the same effect by moving a magnet in and out of a coil of wire.

Faraday described this as a "conversion of magnetism to electricity"; it was

In his electromagnetic rotation experiment, Faraday stood a bar magnet upright in mercury (a conductor of electricity). When the electric current passes through the wire and the mercury, the wire moves freely around the magnet. In the second experiment Faraday used a fixed wire and movable magnet. In this case the upper end of the magnet rotates around the wire. The experiments proved that electric current could produce continuous movement.

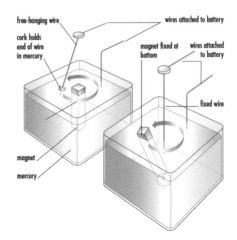

free-hanging wire   wires attached to battery

cork holds end of wire in mercury   magnet fixed at bottom   wires attached to battery

fixed wire

magnet

mercury

the first dynamo, a device for converting mechanical energy to electrical energy. He also found that by rotating a copper disk between the poles of an electromagnet, a steady current was produced between the center of the disk and its edge; in other words, rotary motion had become electricity.

FORMS OF ELECTRICITY

Faraday was a gifted experimenter, but he was also an original thinker who gave careful consideration to what his experiments revealed. Now that he had established that electricity came from several different sources—from friction, lightning, voltaic piles, and electromagnets, for example—it seemed reasonable for him to ask how many kinds of electricity there were and whether they differed.

Was the electricity that was produced by magnetic induction, for example, the same as the electricity produced by a battery? Eventually Faraday was able to demonstrate that "electricity, whatever may be its source, is identical in its nature" by showing that different forms of electricity, however they are produced, behave in similarly predictable ways.

PROVING THE EXISTENCE OF LINES OF FORCE

Faraday knew that an electric current could be produced in a coil by independent and unconnected events in a distant coil, but he wanted to know how this happened. In answering this question he developed field theory, which was based on the concept of lines of force.

For Faraday forces were the important elements of the natural world. In place of the vacuum of space, he imagined there must be lines of force spreading out from centers of force and that connections could be drawn between these centers of force in various ways. Whether space was empty or filled with matter, he once asserted, there were always forces at work, and these forces were always exerted through lines. Later Faraday devised an experiment to prove that these lines of force exist. Sprinkling iron filings on a sheet of paper, he held a magnet underneath. The lines of force could be clearly seen.

This way of thinking led Faraday to argue that there is an underlying harmony or unity in nature, and that all physical and chemical activity is interrelated. He pointed out that only a few years earlier magnetism had been seen as a strange force affecting a few objects only. However, now he believed it had an influence on all objects, and that it must be closely linked with electricity, heat, chemical action, light, crystallization, and the forces holding atoms and molecules together. Faraday felt strongly that at some point he would be able to prove that magnetism also had a bond with gravity.

The strain of thinking about these ideas, and of carrying out so much experimental work, had its effect. In 1839, Faraday's health broke down, and he had to spend three years away from

A photograph of metal filings around a magnet shows the filings forming lines of force spreading out from the north and south poles of the magnet. Faraday imagined that these lines occupied the whole of space. The lines are most dense where the force is strongest, around the ends of the magnet.

his laboratory, traveling to Switzerland to recuperate. He returned to active research in 1845, and carried out a successful experiment in which he found that light could be affected by magnetism. This confirmed his faith in the unity of forces, as it showed that "magnetic force and light were proved to have a relation to each other."

Faraday was less successful with his attempts to link gravity and electricity. "Surely," he wrote in 1849, "this force must be capable of an experimental relation to Electricity, Magnetism, and the other forces." In his attempt to find such links, he dropped samples of copper, iron, bismuth, and other metals from the ceiling of his lecture theater on to a cushion. Although the samples were surrounded by coils of copper wire connected to a sensitive measuring device, no current was ever detected. Nor were any results obtained in 1859 when a 280 pound (127 kg) lead weight was dropped 165 feet (50 m). Yet Faraday was not put off by his failures. "I cannot accept them as conclusive," he insisted. He planned to repeat the experiments with more sensitive instruments, but failing health and memory ended his scientific career in the 1860s.

Faraday was not a natural mathematician and had never had the chance to learn mathematical skills. This was perhaps his greatest weakness as a scientist. It was James Clerk Maxwell (1831–1879), a Scottish physicist, who developed Faraday's ideas into a mathematically sound theory in his *Treatise on Electricity and Magnetism* (1873), and, in so doing, created an account of physics that lasted until Einstein's work in the early 20th century

ELECTRICITY AND INDUSTRY

Faraday's experiments had sown the seeds of a new electrical industry, though it was some time before it became fully established. Batteries powerful enough to drive big motors were still heavy and expensive, so in transport the steam engine continued to be a more efficient method of powering vehicles. Electric trains were produced, but they were very slow.

Dynamos provided a useful source of electrical power, first in the electroplating industry, where the first large dynamo for electroplating was installed in Birmingham, England, in the 1840s.

Electrical lighting for public and domestic use was at first provided by arc lamps. Davy and Faraday had both demonstrated these at their lectures; arc lamps produced a "continuous spark" between two carbon rods but were unpredictable and harsh, and gas lamps were still preferred by many people. By the 1880s, the development of efficient generators, such as steam turbines, meant that electricity could be produced on a much greater scale than before. At the same time, the invention of the incandescent light bulb by American physicist Thomas Edison (1847–1931) in 1879 brought about a breakthrough in electric lighting. The first public power station for electric lighting was opened in London in January 1882; another opened in September in New York City.

Faraday's induction ring was the first transformer, a device that transfers current from one circuit to another with an increase or decrease in voltage. At first electricity could not be transmitted any

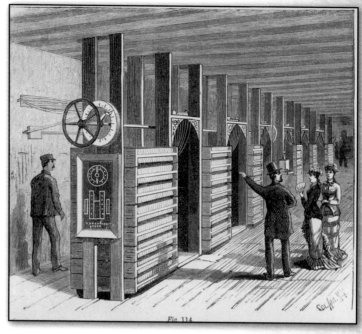

Fig. 114

Faraday's discoveries led in time to the rise of the electrical industry, based on commercial development of the dynamo. Shown above are the huge generators of New York's first electric lighting station. This opened in 1882, following Thomas Edison's invention of the incandescent light bulb in 1879.

distance, but once transformers were introduced, it meant that the voltage could be increased so it could be transmitted over a long distance, then decreased for domestic or public use at the other end.

LECTURES AND PUBLIC SCIENCE

Faraday's entire career was spent at the Royal Institution. Initially the Institution was financed by private donations of money, and it soon developed a program to encourage both theoretical and practical aspects of science. Practical projects included the invention of the miners' safety lamp known as the Davy Lamp and advising the government on the purity of the water supply.

Faraday played a key role in the Institution's efforts to popularize science, starting the Christmas lectures for children in 1827. The aim was to make the lectures entertaining as well as instructive, and great emphasis was placed on practical demonstrations. It was a winning formula. Faraday himself delivered 19 series of lectures. His best-known course was published as *The Chemical History of a Candle* (1861), which is still in print.

In 1826, Faraday also began a series of Friday evening lectures given by working scientists about recent developments in their fields. From the start, they attracted large numbers—some of Faraday's own lectures were listened to by audiences of more than 1,000 people.

Faraday lecturing at the Royal Institution. Prince Albert, husband of Queen Victoria, and two of their four sons are seated at center front. Faraday's Christmas lectures for children proved a popular and enduring formula; they are still delivered today.

A GREAT MAN IN DECLINE

By the end of his life, Faraday was the most famous scientist in Britain, but he refused to accept any official public post. His health began to fail once more after 1855, and he was forced to give up any experimental work. He became forgetful and confused; he may have developed Alzheimer's disease. In 1860, he confessed in a letter to a fellow chemist: "I do not remember the order of things....I tear up my letters, for I write nonsense. I cannot spell or write a line continuously. Whether I shall recover...I do not know...."

Faraday was a deeply religious man. He and his wife belonged to the Sandemanian Church. This was a branch of the Presbyterian church, which had been founded in Scotland in the 18th century. Its followers led a simple life; they believed that it was against the word of the Bible to accumulate riches and pursue worldly reward. For this reason, Faraday turned down the offer of a knighthood from the English queen Victoria (1819–1901). This was a high personal honor, given in recognition of his services to science, and would have

An early photograph, known as a daguerreotype, showing Michael Faraday and his wife, Sarah.

meant that he was known as Sir Michael Faraday. But he stated that he preferred to remain "plain Mr Faraday to the end." He died on August 25, 1867.

PERIODIC TABLE OF ELEMENTS

The periodic table organizes all the chemical elements into a simple chart according to the physical and chemical properties of their atoms. The elements are arranged by atomic number from 1 to 118. The atomic number is based on the number of protons in the nucleus of the atom. The atomic mass is the combined mass of protons and neutrons in the nucleus. Each element has a chemical symbol that is an abbreviation of its name. In some cases, such as potassium,

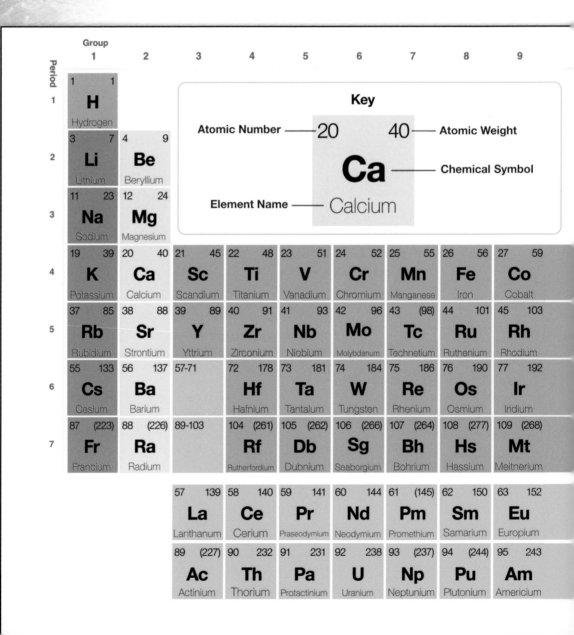

the symbol is an abbreviation of its Latin name ("K" stands for kalium). The name by which the element is commonly known is given in full underneath the symbol. The last item in the element box is the atomic mass. This is the average mass of an atom of the element.

Scientists have arranged the elements into vertical columns called groups and horizontal rows called periods. Elements in any one group all have the same number of electrons in their outer shell and have similar chemical properties. Periods represent the increasing number of electrons it takes to fill the inner and outer shells and become stable. When all the spaces have been filled (Group 18 atoms have all their shells filled) the next period begins.

10	11	12	13	14	15	16	17	18
								2 4 **He** Helium
			5 11 **B** Boron	6 12 **C** Carbon	7 14 **N** Nitrogen	8 16 **O** Oxygen	9 19 **F** Fluorine	10 20 **Ne** Neon
			13 27 **Al** Aluminum	14 28 **Si** Silicon	15 31 **P** Phosphorus	16 32 **S** Sulfur	17 35 **Cl** Chlorine	18 40 **Ar** Argon
28 59 **Ni** Nickel	29 64 **Cu** Copper	30 65 **Zn** Zinc	31 70 **Ga** Gallium	32 73 **Ge** Germanium	33 75 **As** Arsenic	34 79 **Se** Selenium	35 80 **Br** Bromine	36 84 **Kr** Krypton
46 106 **Pd** Palladium	47 108 **Ag** Silver	48 112 **Cd** Cadmium	49 115 **In** Indium	50 119 **Sn** Tin	51 122 **Sb** Antimony	52 128 **Te** Tellurium	53 127 **I** Iodine	54 131 **Xe** Xenon
78 195 **Pt** Platinum	79 197 **Au** Gold	80 201 **Hg** Mercury	81 204 **Tl** Thallium	82 207 **Pb** Lead	83 209 **Bi** Bismuth	84 (209) **Po** Polonium	85 (210) **At** Astatine	86 (222) **Rn** Radon
110 (281) **Ds** Darmstadtium	111 (280) **Rg** Roentgenium	112 (285) **Cn** Copernicium	113 (284) **Uut** Ununtrium	114 (289) **Fl** Flerovium	115 (288) **Uup** Ununpentium	116 (293) **Lv** Livermorium	117 (294) **Uus** Ununseptium	118 (294) **Uuo** Ununoctium

64 157 **Gd** Gadolinium	65 159 **Tb** Terbium	66 163 **Dy** Dysprosium	67 165 **Ho** Holmium	68 167 **Er** Erbium	69 169 **Tm** Thulium	70 173 **Yb** Ytterbium	71 175 **Lu** Lutetium
96 (247) **Cm** Curium	97 (247) **Bk** Berkelium	98 (251) **Cf** Californium	99 (252) **Es** Einsteinium	100 (257) **Fm** Fermium	101 (258) **Md** Mendelevium	102 (259) **No** Nobelium	103 (262) **Lr** Lawrencium

	SCIENTIFIC BACKGROUND		POLITICAL AND CULTURAL BACKGROUND	

Before 1800

Dutch physicist Peter van Musschenbroek (1692–1761) invents the Leiden jar, which stores an electrical charge

Italian physiologist Luigi Galvani (1737–1798) claims to have discovered "animal electricity"

American-born scientist Benjamin Thompson (later Count Rumford) (1753–1814) founds the Royal Institution in London

1788 The first shipload of English convicts lands at Botany Bay in Australia; others join them and they move to nearby Port Jackson (later renamed Sydney)

1800

1800 Italian physicist Alessandro Volta (1745–1827) invents the electric battery; water is decomposed into hydrogen and oxygen

1801 Virginia lawyer Thomas Jefferson (1743–1826), who drafted the 1776 Declaration of Independence, becomes third president of the United States

1807 English physicist and physician Thomas Young (1773–1829) revives the wave theory of light first proposed by English scientist Robert Hooke (1635–1703) and Dutch physicist and mathematician Christiaan Huygens (1629–1695)

1808 English scientist Humphry Davy (1778–1829) connects battery wires to two carbon rods to create the "arc lamp"

1808 Napoleon's brother Joseph Bonaparte (1768–1844) seizes the Spanish throne; despite continued opposition from his subjects, he will reign until 1813

1810

1818 The border between Canada and the United States is fixed

1820

1820 Danish physicist Hans Christian Oersted (1777–1851) demonstrates the magnetic effect of an electric current

1821 Nationalist Greeks begin their battle for independence from the Turkish Ottoman Empire; a Greek kingdom is eventually established in 1832

1822 The German folklorists Jacob Ludwig Carl Grimm (1785–1863) and his brother Wilhelm Carl Grimm (1786–1859) complete the third volume of their collection of folk stories, *Grimm's Fairy Tales*

1821 Faraday establishes existence of electromagnetic rotation

1825 Faraday discovers benzene

1827 German physicist Georg Simon Ohm (1789–1854) publishes Ohm's Law, which describes the relationship between electrical current, voltage, and resistance

1827 American bird artist John James Audubon (1785–1851) begins publication of *Birds of America*, which will eventually consist of more than 1,000 lifesize drawings

1830

1831 Faraday demonstrates electromagnetic induction

1833 Faraday establishes two laws of electrolysis

1830 American scientist Joseph Henry (1797–1878) discovers electromagnetic induction; but does not publish his work immediately

1830 Mormonism is founded in the United States by American religious leader Joseph Smith (1805–1844)

1835 More than 12,000 European-origin South Africans (Afrikaners), protesting at-policies under British rule that include a ban on slavery, begin their "Great Trek" northeast from Cape Colony to settle new areas; they later found Transvaal (1852) and the Orange Free State (1854)

1835 Faraday describes "Faraday rotation," or how polarized light is rotated in a magnetic field

1840

1845 Irish-born Scottish physicist and mathematician William Thomson, Lord Kelvin (1824–1907) gives a mathematical explanation for "lines of force"

1844 Faraday describes his force-field theory—that a web of lines of gravitational force spreads out from the Sun and runs throughout the universe—in a lecture at the Royal Institution

1846 The Mexican–American War begins in a dispute over American expansion in Texas; Mexico renounces claims to Texas in 1848

1846 The potato famine in Ireland leads to a massive increase in the numbers of people emigrating from there to the United States over the following two years

1850

1852 After widespread revolution throughout Europe, Louis Napoleon (1808–1873) restores the French empire when he becomes Emperor Napoleon III

1857 Muslim and Hindu troops stage a series of mutinies against British rule in India; these are suppressed, and in 1858 authority in India is transferred from the East India Company to the British monarchy

1860

1861 Faraday publishes one of his best-known lectures, *The Chemical History of a Candle*, which he has delivered at the Royal Institution

1864 Scottish physicist James Clerk Maxwell (1831–1879) publishes "A Dynamical Theory of the Electromagnetic Field," which describes the main features of electricity, magnetism, and light in four mathematical equations

1867 Russia sells Alaska to American secretary-of-state William Henry Seward (1801–1872); for a time "Seward's Folly" remains uneconomical, until gold is discovered there in 1896

1869 The first transcontinental railroad runs from Sacramento, California, to Omaha, Nebraska, cutting travel time from San Francisco to New York from a minimum of three months to just eight days

After 1865

1873 Maxwell publishes his *Treatise on Electricity and Magnetism*, which predicts that electromagnetic waves might be generated in a laboratory

1879 American inventor Thomas Alva Edison (1847–1931) invents the incandescent electric light bulb

1887 As predicted by Maxwell, German physicist Heinrich Hertz (1857–1894) succeeds in generating electromagnetic waves, which he finds behave like light waves but have different wavelengths

1876 At the Battle of Little Big Horn, a U.S. cavalry force under Lieutenant-Colonel George Armstrong Custer (1839–1876) is massacred by Dakota Sioux led by Tatanka Iyotake, known as Sitting Bull (1834–1890)

acid Substance that dissolves in water to form hydrogen ions (H+). Acids are neutralized by alkalis and have a pH below 7.

alkali Substance that dissolves in water to form hydroxide ions (OH-). Alkalis have a pH greater than 7 and will react with acids to form salts.

alkali metals Those metals that form Group 1 of the periodic table.

alkaline-earth metals Those metals that form Group 2 of the periodic table.

allotrope A different form of an element in which the atoms are arranged in a different structure.

alloy A metallic substance that contains two or more metals. An alloy may also be made of a metal and a small amount of a nonmetal. Steel, for example, is an alloy of iron and carbon.

alumina Aluminum oxide, Al_2O_3. The most common aluminum ore.

amalgams Alloys that contain mercury.

anion Negatively charged ion.

atom The smallest independent building block of matter. All substances are made of atoms.

atomic mass The number of protons and neutrons in an atom's nucleus.

atomic number The number of protons in a nucleus.

base Any substance that produces hydroxide ions, OH-, is a base. All alkalis are bases.

boiling point The temperature at which a liquid turns into a gas.

bond A chemical connection between atoms.

brass An alloy of copper and zinc.

bronze Alloy made of copper and tin.

by-product A substance that is produced when another material is made.

catalyst A substance that speeds up a chemical reaction but is left unchanged at the end of the reaction.

cation A positively charged ion.

chemical equation Symbols and numbers that show how reactants change into products during a chemical reaction.

chemical formula The letters and numbers that represent a chemical compound, such as "H_2O" for water.

chemical reaction A process in which atoms of different elements join or break apart to form new substances.

chemical symbol The letters that represent a chemical, such as "Cl" for chlorine or "Na" for sodium.

combination reaction A reaction in which two or more reactants combine to form one product.

combustion The reaction that causes burning. Combustion is generally a reaction with oxygen in the air.

compound Substance made from more than one element and which has undergone a chemical reaction.

compress To reduce in size or volume by squeezing or exerting pressure.

conductor A substance that carries electricity and heat.

corrosion The slow wearing away of metals or solids by chemical attack.

covalent bond Bond in which atoms share one or more electrons.

crystal A solid made of regular repeating patterns of atoms.

crystal lattice The regular repeated structure found in crystalline solids.

density The mass of substance in a unit of volume.

deposit A mineral vein or ore inside another rock.

displacement reaction A reaction that occurs when a more reactive atom replaces a less reactive atom in a compound.

dissolve To form a solution.

doping Process by which the properties of semiconductors are adjusted by adding tiny amounts of metalloids.

ductile Describes materials that can be stretched into a thin wire. Many metals are ductile.

elastic Describes a substance that returns to its original shape after being stretched.

electricity A stream of electrons or other charged particles moving through a substance.

electrolysis A method of separating elements in ionic compounds by dissolving the compound in an appropriate solvent and passing an electric current through the solution.

electrolyte Liquid containing ions that carries a current between electrodes.

electron A tiny negatively charged particle that moves around the nucleus of an atom.

electronegativity The power of an atom to attract an electron. Nonmetals, which have only a few spaces in their outer shell, are the most electronegative. Metals, which have several empty spaces in their outer shell, are the least electronegative elements. These metals tend to lose electrons in chemical reactions. Metals of this type are termed electropositive.

element A material that cannot be broken up into simpler ingredients. Elements contain only one type of atom.

energy level The electron shells of an atom each represent a different energy level. Those closest to the nucleus have the lowest energy.

galena Lead sulfide (PbS), the most common mineral containing lead.

geologist Scientist who studies rocks and minerals.

group A column of related elements in the periodic table.

Hall–Héroult process Process for producing large quantities of aluminum.

hematite A compound of iron and oxygen. Hematite is the most common iron ore.

hydrogen bond A weak dipole attraction that always involves a hydrogen atom.

insulator A substance that does not transfer an electric current or heat.

intermolecular bonds The bonds that hold molecules together. These bonds are weaker than those between atoms in a molecule.

intramolecular bond Strong bond between atoms in a molecule.

ion An atom that has lost or gained one or more electrons.

ionic bond Bond in which one atom gives one or more electrons to another atom.

ionic compound Compound made of ionized atoms.

ionization The formation of ions by adding or removing electrons from atoms.

isotope Atoms of a given element must have the same number of protons but can have different numbers of neutrons. These different versions of the same element are called isotopes.

liquid Substance in which particles are loosely bonded and are able to move freely around each other.

lubricant A substance that helps surfaces slide past each other.

magnet A piece of iron, nickel, or cobalt that produces a magnetic force.

malleable Describes a material that can be hammered into different shapes without breaking. Metals are malleable.

melting point The temperature at which a solid changes into a liquid. When a liquid changes into a solid, this same temperature is called the freezing point.

metal An element that is solid, shiny, malleable, ductile, and conductive.

metallic bond Bond in which outer electrons are free to move in the spaces between the atoms.

metalloid Elements that have properties of both metals and nonmetals.

metallurgy The science and technology of metals and their alloys, including methods of extraction and use.

microprocessor A tiny silicon chip that contains all the electronic circuits used to run a computer.

mineral A naturally occurring compound, such as those that make up rocks and soil.

mole The amount of any substance that contains the same number of atoms as in 12 grams of carbon-12 atoms. This number is 6.022×10^{23}.

molecule Two or more bonded atoms that form a substance with specific properties.

neutron One of the particles that make up the nucleus of an atom. Neutrons do not have any electric charge.

nucleus The central part of an atom. The nucleus contains protons and neutrons. The exception is hydrogen, which contains only one proton.

ore A mineral that contains valuable amounts of materials such as copper, sulfur, or tin.

oxidation state A number used to describe how many electrons an atom has lost or gained.

oxide Compound that includes oxygen.

periodic table A table of elements arranged by increasing atomic number (proton number).

phase change A change from one state to another.

potash Potassium carbonate (K_2CO_3). Contains potassium, carbon, and oxygen.

pressure The force produced by pressing on something.

proton A positively charged particle found in an atom's nucleus.

quartz A crystalline form of silica, silicon dioxide (SiO_2).

rare-earth metals Metals that form two rows of elements—the actinides and the lanthanides—below the main body of the periodic table.

reactivity The tendency of an element to react chemically with other elements.

reducing agent A compound that gives away electrons during a chemical reaction.

refine To purify a metal by getting rid of other unwanted elements.

relative atomic mass A measure of the mass of an atom compared with the mass of another atom. The values used are the same as those for atomic mass.

relative molecular mass The sum of all the atomic masses of the atoms in a molecule.

salt A compound made from positive and negative ions that forms when an alkali reacts with an acid.

semiconductor A substance that conducts heat and electricity but only in certain circumstances.

shell The orbit of an electron. Each shell can contain a specific number of electrons and no more.

smelting Method for purifying metals from their ores.

solid State of matter in which particles are held in a rigid arrangement.

specific heat capacity The amount of heat required to change the temperature of a specified amount of a substance by 1°C (1.8°F).

standard conditions Normal room temperature and pressure.

state The form that matter takes—either a solid, a liquid, or a gas.

steel An alloy of iron and carbon.

subatomic particles Particles that are smaller than an atom.

temperature A measure of how fast molecules are moving.

transition metals Those metals that make up groups 3 through 12 of the periodic table.

valence A measure of the number of bonds an atom can form with other atoms.

valence electrons The electrons in the outer shell of an atom.

voltage The force that pushes electrons through an electric circuit.

American Association for the
Advancement of Science (AAAS)
1200 New York Avenue NW
Washington, DC 20005
(202) 326-6400
Web site: http://www.aaas.org
Founded in 1848, AAAS serves some 261
affiliated societies and academies of
science and publishes the peer-
reviewed general science journal
Science. The non-profit AAAS is open
to all and fulfills its mission to advance
science and serve society through ini-
tiatives that include science policy,
international programs, science education, and public understanding of
science.

American Chemical Society (ACS)
1155 Sixteenth Street NW
Washington, DC 20036
(800) 227-5558
Web site: http://www.acs.org/content/
acs/en.html
With more than 163,000 members, the
American Chemical Society (ACS) is
the world's largest scientific society
and one of the world's leading sources
of authoritative scientific information.
A nonprofit organization, ACS is the
premier professional home for chemists, chemical engineers, and related
professions around the globe. ACS is
committed to improving people's
lives through the transforming power
of chemistry.

Brookhaven National Laboratory
Chemistry Department, Bldg. 555A

P.O. Box 5000
Upton, NY 11973-5000
(631) 344-4301
Web site: http://www.bnl.gov/chemistry/
default.asp
The Chemistry Department of the
Brookhaven National Laboratory
conducts basic research in the chemical sciences on subjects ranging
from nuclear processes shortly after
the big bang to medical imaging and
many topics in between. Major topics of the department's research
include: catalysis and surface science; charge transfer for energy
conversion; chemistry with ionizing
radiation; nanoscience; combustion;
nuclear chemistry; and experimental
and theoretical programs studying
imaging and neuroscience.

Journal of Biological Chemistry
c/o ASBMB
11200 Rockville Pike, Suite 302
Rockville, MD 20852-3110
(240) 283-6620
Web site: http://www.jbc.org
The *Journal of Biological Chemistry* publishes papers based on original
research that is judged to make a
novel and important contribution to
understanding the molecular and
cellular basis of biological processes.

National Science Foundation
Division of Chemistry
4201 Wilson Boulevard
Arlington, VA 22230
(703) 292-5111

Web site: http://www.nsf.gov/div/index
.jsp?div=CHE

The mission of the Division of
Chemistry is to promote the health
of academic chemistry and to
enable basic research and education in the chemical sciences. The
division supports research in all
traditional areas of chemistry and
in multidisciplinary fields that
draw upon the chemical sciences.
The division also supports projects
that help build infrastructure,
workforce, and partnerships that
advance the chemical sciences.

Nobel Prize in Chemistry
Nobel Media AB
Sturegatan 14
Box 5232
SE-102 45 Stockholm
Sweden
Web site: http://www.nobelprize.org/
nobel_prizes/chemistry

The Chemistry Prize has been awarded to
163 Nobel laureates since 1901.
Chemistry was the second prize area
that Alfred Nobel mentioned in his
will. The Nobel Prize in Chemistry is
awarded by the Royal Swedish
Academy of Sciences, Stockholm,
Sweden.

Royal Society of Chemistry (RSC)
Burlington House

Piccadilly, London W1J 0BA
England
Web site: http://www.rsc.org

The RSC is the largest organization in
Europe for advancing the chemical
sciences. Supported by a worldwide
network of members and an international publishing business, its
activities span education, confer-
ences, science policy, and the
promotion of chemistry to the
public.

Science Magazine
1200 New York Avenue NW
Washington, DC 20005
(202) 326-6550
Web site: http://www.sciencemag.org

Founded in 1880 on $10,000 of seed money
from the American inventor Thomas
Edison, *Science* has grown to become
the world's leading outlet for scientific
news, commentary, and cutting-edge
research.

WEB SITES

Due to the changing nature of Internet
links, Rosen Publishing has developed
an online list of Web sites related to the
subject of this book. This site is updated
regularly. Please use this link to access
the list:

http://www.rosenlinks.com/CORE/Metal

Brown, Theodore E., et al. *Chemistry: The Central Science*. Upper Saddle River, NJ: Prentice Hall, 2011.

Chang, Raymond, and Kenneth A. Goldsby. *Chemistry*. New York, NY: McGraw-Hill Science/Engineering/Math, 2012.

Curran, Greg. *Homework Helpers: Chemistry*. Pompton Plains, NJ: Career Press, 2011.

Gilbert, Thomas R. *Chemistry: The Science in Context*. New York, NY: W.W. Norton & Co., 2011.

Gray, Theodore. *The Elements: A Visual Exploration of Every Known Atom in the Universe*. New York, NY: Black Dog & Leventhal Publishers, 2012.

Gray, Theodore. *The Photographic Card Deck of the Elements: With Big Beautiful Photographs of All 118 Elements in the Periodic Table*. New York, NY: Black Dog & Leventhal Publishers, 2010.

Gray, Theodore, and Simon Quellen Field. *Theodore Gray's Elements Vault: Treasures of the Periodic Table with Removable Archival Documents and Real Element Samples—Including Pure Gold!* New York, NY: Black Dog & Leventhal Publishers, 2011.

Jackson, Tom. *The Elements: An Illustrated History of the Periodic Table*. New York, NY: Shelter Harbor Press, 2012.

Kean, Sam. *The Disappearing Spoon: and Other True Tales of Madness, Love, and the History of the World from the Periodic Table of the Elements*. New York, NY: Back Bay Books, 2011.

Mikulecky, Peter J., et al. *Chemistry Workbook for Dummies*. Hoboken, NJ: Wiley Publishing, 2008.

Moore, John T. *Chemistry for Dummies*. Hoboken, NJ: For Dummies, 2011.

Silberberg, Martin. *Chemistry: The Molecular Nature of Matter and Change*. New York, NY: McGraw-Hill Science/Engineering/Math, 2011.

Timberlake, Karen C. *Chemistry: An Introduction to General, Organic, and Biological Chemistry*. Upper Saddle River, NJ: Prentice Hall, 2011.

PHOTO CREDITS